EGGin'

DAVID ROSE Cooks on the
Big Green Egg

EGGin'

DAVID ROSE Cooks on the
Big Green Egg®

DAVID ROSE

Photography by

KATHRYN McCRARY

Andrews McMeel
PUBLISHING®

Carol and Aston Rose (Mom and Dad),
this book is for you! I dedicate this book
to my parents—without them, there is
no me. You two have unconditionally loved
and supported me through thick and thin on
all of my dreams, no matter how big, small,
or crazy. My love for cooking and great food,
dashing good looks, and integrity comes from
you two. Thank you for being my parents!

CONTENTS

Chapter 6: Breakin' the Fast (BREAKFAST)

Chapter 7: Libations (ADULTS ONLY)

Chapter 8: Happy Ending (DESSERT)

INTRODUCTION:
EGGIN' WITH DAVID

Food and I have always had a lifelong love affair . . . meat, poultry, seafood, desserts, you name it. If it tastes good, sign me up. But honestly, the eternal torch I carry for grilled and smoked meats shines a whole lot brighter than the rest. My ears perk up at the insatiable sizzle when a well-marbled rib eye hits the open flame. My taste buds dance in anticipation from the aroma of perfectly marinated Jamaican jerk chicken wafting from a roadside eatery's smoke shack. The spicy, warm, and sweet flavors indicative of pimento wood smoking capture my heart and soul and don't let go. My first bite of a proper pulled pork sandwich expertly blends seasoned bark and unctuous fat that literally melts in your mouth. The barbecue sauce from baby back ribs dribbles down my cheek, my shirt, my pants, then my shoes, and all I can do is smile. Because GREAT BARBECUE is well worth the dry-cleaning expense, and it's the thing that dreams are made of.

When you're talking barbecue, grilling, smoking, versatility, and quality, three words come to mind: "Feed ME, please?!" Well . . . that, too, but what I really mean is "BIG GREEN EGG"! Yes, the Big Green Egg, the EGG, the Ultimate Cooking Experience, "that green dome smoker thingy that makes insanely delicious smoked meats." You know what I'm talking about. But before I go deeper down the rabbit hole of the countless reasons why I love the Big Green Egg, let's start from the beginning.

Thirty-nine years ago in New Jersey, I was born the last of eight children to Carol and Aston Rose, Jamaican immigrants who ventured to the States in search of better opportunities for themselves and their children. Mom was one of thirteen children. She was born and raised in Heart Ease, a quaint region in the Saint Thomas parish of Jamaica, bordering the Blue Mountains—a place rich in family and religious faith and with no lack of good food or unconditional love for their fellow man. Dad was one of seven children, a city boy from Kingston, the capital of Jamaica. Needless to say, if you ask how many cousins, aunts, and uncles I have, I will promptly answer: "A LOT!"

Mom was a waitress at my uncle Vin's restaurant in Kingston. Every day Dad would come to the restaurant straight from work and ask for my mother to wait on him. (Smooth, right? I know.) So after being a regular guest at the family restaurant for quite some time, I guess Mom got tired of waiting for Dad to ask her out, so she made the first move, and they went out on their first date. And as they say, "The rest is history."

I'm sharing all this to emphasize that delicious food has always been an integral part of my life, starting with initially bringing my parents together. Food helped them find love all those years ago in my uncle's cozy restaurant in Kingston. So you could then probably say I'm the product of "food lovemaking" (slow eye wink)! Some of my earliest, fondest memories I can recollect involve food in some way, shape, or form.

The food of Jamaica is a culinary melting pot, with the indigenous Arawak American Indian from Greater Antilles and South America, inhabitants from Africa, South America, India, Spain, China, England, and many other places far and wide. The cultural influences run deep; the curries of India run through my veins as well as the tongue-numbing jerk chicken. The cornucopia of food from the great island of Jamaica is the cuisine I was raised on. I identify fun and great times with it. I'm in love with it.

When Mom and Dad came to the US in 1979, they both took on jobs as chefs. Dad was a chef at a monastery for nuns, and Mom was a chef at a nursing home. As a kid, I remember the days when they would take me to work with them. I was no more than six or seven years old and recall being totally mesmerized by the symphony of cooking and multitasking in their respective kitchens. I didn't realize it at the time, but these early memories would plant the seeds for my own culinary career.

The very first job I had in hospitality was at a hotel in Englewood, New Jersey. I started out as a busboy and room service attendant. Although I'm not sure of the legality of delivering alcohol to hotel guests as a thirteen-year-old, the idea of making $30 to $60 in cash tips a night was pretty amazing. From there I was promoted to a server and actually took restaurant guests' orders. It was from this point that I started to really understand, appreciate, and enjoy providing great service and exceptional dining experiences. The guests trusted me to be their tour guide across the menu and help them with all of their food and drink needs. I took great pride in my work, and that pride has followed me throughout my career.

In my late teens and early twenties I hit a nice little groove as a bartender at several restaurants, nightclubs, country clubs, and catering events. It allowed me to be creative through crafting cocktails with a wide array of spirits. At the time, my older cousin Omar was a student at the prestigious Morehouse College in Atlanta, Georgia. And at his urging, I decided to come down and visit for my twenty-first birthday. I was smitten with the emerging and fast-moving city. Atlanta was so rich in culture, history, food, and nightlife. I was hooked, and I was ready for the next chapter of my life to begin there.

A couple months later, in the summer of 2003, I packed up my cherry-red Mustang with all of my belongings and embarked on my new journey. I arrived and instantly submerged myself in the hospitality industry by serving and bartending at different restaurants, clubs, and bars. I loved bartending, but I knew there was something more out there for me, a higher calling. I just wasn't quite sure what it was at the time.

I've told this story a thousand times, but I'll tell it again because, after all, it's not every day you write your first cookbook partnered with Big Green Egg. I remember it like it was yesterday. I was home watching TV, and I heard a commercial say, "Come to Le Cordon Bleu and realize your culinary dreams!" I don't know whether it was the background music from the commercial that got my attention, or what, but I just knew I had to visit the Le Cordon Bleu Atlanta campus and realize my "culinary dream." I always loved to cook for myself, family, and friends, especially at the occasional impromptu summer barbecue. I learned how to grill at the tender age of eight, when Dad handed me a pair of tongs and said, "Don't let the chicken burn," and walked away. I had always loved to cook but had never considered doing it professionally. That commercial spoke volumes to me that day.

Upon entering the campus, talking to the admissions department, taking a tour, and reading the curriculum, I instantly knew that this was my future and food was my purpose. I immediately enrolled that day for the fall semester. There was something about the culinary school that gave me such a hunger for knowledge, learning, creativity, and aspiration to get as much as I could out of the program. It didn't feel like school but more like I was training for my destiny, similar to Rocky training for his rematch against Apollo Creed. I was a sponge and wanted to absorb as much information and learn as much as I could.

I graduated from Le Cordon Bleu in 2006, at the top of my class, summa cum laude with honors and a 4.0 GPA. That was one of the happiest and most prideful days for my parents and myself. I was ready to go out, take my talents on the road, and spread my wings to fly. My first job out of culinary school was at a very well-renowned hotel in Atlanta. I worked the fish station, meat station, room service, and garde-manger (salad and cold apps) station. I appreciated and enjoyed the on-the-job training, and I actually learned a lot while working there. But I started to hear that voice in my head again, telling me there was something else out there. I worked at the hotel for a year, but eventually I sat down with my boss, the executive chef. I told him that I was giving my two weeks' notice. I explained to him that I aspired to do my own thing, catering and providing personal culinary services. He pretty much told me I was crazy, that this would be the single biggest mistake of my culinary career and I would immediately regret it. All I could say was, "Chef, I'm sorry, but I have to respectfully disagree." And I went on my way.

It was a slow go at first, but I started to amass a pretty respectable client list consisting of lawyers, doctors, families, and professional athletes.

And so, Rose Events—catering, private dinners, and providing personal meal plan services—was born. I did very well, and I was happy.

A couple years later in 2010, I pulled the trigger on my first motorcycle. I rode motorcycles off and on throughout my twenties but never actually owned my own. So I treated myself . . . Why not? A 2010 Harley-Davidson Fat Boy Lo, and boy, do I love that motorcycle!

Which leads me to my first encounter with Big Green Egg. Around 2014, the staff at Le Cordon Bleu reached out to me to do some in-classroom cooking demonstrations for their current students and to share my story. I jumped at the opportunity to give back to my alma mater, which had given so much to me. After reconnecting with old college friends and faculty, I was tapped to help participate at a Big Green Egg event being held at the old EGG HQ. I was hypnotized by the ease, efficiency, and awesome food the EGG produced. Up until that very moment, I'd never cooked on such a high-performance grill, and I marveled at the many different capabilities it had. I playfully always call the EGG "the Swiss Army knife of grills," because this grill does it all.

I attended my first Big Green EGGtoberfest that year in 2014. I was blown away by the comradery of the EGGheads, the broad bandwidth of exciting and original dishes they created with the EGGs, and the sheer fun everybody was having bonding over their mutual love for the Big Green Egg. I was instantly hooked! I had a great conversation with the Big Green Egg marketing lead and started out with my very first large Big Green Egg. I've never experienced the joy and excitement of bringing a newborn infant home. However, I'm pretty sure bringing your first brand-new EGG home isn't too far off from that excitement!

From that point, I started to do more events with Big Green Egg and participated in EGGtoberfest 2015 as a culinary partner. That year and every year after at EGGtoberfest, I aim to feed the droves of EGGheads nontraditional barbecue and grilled fare off of the EGG. I continuously push myself to see what hasn't been done on the EGG. For several years, I had the pleasure of being a Big Green Egg culinary instructor at "the Mothership," Big Green Egg corporate HQ. I taught the way of the EGG and cooked for various corporations, business meetings, and even my own branded business partnered with Big Green Egg for events. It never ceases to amaze me when people compliment my cooking and say, "You really made that on the EGG?" To which I reply with a happy grin, "Yep!"

During my time at Big Green Egg as a guest culinary instructor, I became lifelong friends with a lot of the staff, from the warehouse workers, to the marketing team, to the president—and I even cooked for Big Green Egg founder Ed Fisher when he sat in on one of my classes. He gave me the highest compliment I could ever hope to receive. He told me, "David, I've been doing this EGG thing for a while, and you even got me excited about the Big Green Egg during your class!" To which I replied, in a voice as cool as I could muster in the moment, "Thanks, Ed!" (Nailed it!)

Fast-forward to 2017, when I had the pleasure of competing on a little TV show called *Food Network Star*, season 13. What a crazy roller-coaster ride being on that show was, trying to meet challenges like "Cook a meal that describes your culinary point of view, have it be Christmas themed, you must use bananas in the recipe, and you have fifteen minutes to cook it and five seconds to describe your dish at the end in front of a live studio audience." Blank stare. *You want me to do what, Bobby Flay?!* But seriously, I absolutely loved showcasing on that show what my cooking style and I were all about. I competed with my moniker "the Biker Chef," because food and motorcycles are two of my biggest passions. I made long-lasting friendships, and even though I didn't win the show, I had the chance to compete against *Iron Chef* legend Bobby Flay. So that's a pretty cool consolation prize, right? You'll even find the recipe I cooked against him on page 96.

Since competing on *Food Network Star*, I refused to let that loss define where my career went from there. I hustled, dug deep, networked, and committed myself to pursuing the TV culinary industry even more. Where I'm at in my career today is a true testament to my hard work and humility and never giving up on my dreams. And maybe a little help from my biceps too. I appear regularly as a guest chef on several TV programs, and I work as a brand ambassador for many amazing national brands. I'm thankful for it all, but the road always leads me back to Big Green Egg. I've been all over the country to different national events, filmings, and EGGfests. I even had the honor of hosting the first weekend-long virtual Big Green Egg EGGtoberfest in 2020.

The Big Green Egg community is an international community of EGGheads, chefs, and backyard warriors. The EGG is the secret weapon in my grilling arsenal. I've become very proficient and more creative while using the EGG to grill, bake, roast, cold smoke, hot smoke, and everything in between. It's my happy place, and its versatile applications give me everything I need to make any meal my heart and stomach desire. When you're using the Big Green Egg, it's more than just grillin' . . . It's EGGin'! So come on in, get comfortable, and stay awhile. I hope you brought your appetite!

CHAPTER

1

EGGIN' 101

This chapter is all about the tools, EGGcessories, EGG setups, ingredients, tips, tricks, and DOs and DON'Ts that I use whenever I'm EGGin' on the one and only Big Green Egg. In my humble opinion the EGG is the most versatile charcoal grill and smoker in the world . . . And the world is a pretty big place! To fully understand the Big Green Egg, let's start from its inception.

What Is the Big Green EGG?

The Big Green Egg is a kamado-style grill. The name *kamado* is the Japanese word for "stove." It's a traditional Japanese wood- or charcoal-fueled cookstove and works with a vent system. The kamado works off of air circulation, so the more air that's allowed in, the hotter it runs, and the less air that's circulated, the cooler it runs. The kamado has been in existence for many centuries and performs a cooking method like no other.

Big Green Egg founder Ed Fisher had the insight and creativity to fashion a grill/smoker after the kamado, and the Big Green Egg was born. He describes it like this: "The Big Green Egg is a simple yet highly efficient blend of ancient tradition, modern technology, and unmatched quality . . . making it the highest-quality, easiest-to-use outdoor cooker you'll ever own!" (I couldn't have said better myself!) Constructed from state-of-the-art ceramics, the EGG can handle temperatures up to 750°F. It's perfect for baking pizzas and searing steaks, among many other foods that require high heat for cooking. If you can grill it, smoke it, roast it, or bake it . . . you can EGG it!

Temperature control is one of the things I find that really separates the EGG into a category all by itself, because of its ease and efficiency. The rEGGulator vent cap (the cap on the top of the EGG) controls the amount of air flowing through the airtight ceramic cooking chamber (the food cooks in the dome). The ceramic cooking chamber retains heat and keeps food moist in the EGG. The Big Green EGG patented precision-flow draft door (the sliding draft door at the bottom of the EGG) controls the amount of air entering the firebox. The rEGGulator vent cap and draft door work in tandem to hone in on the exact temperature you want for your desired cooking application. All of these features give you "the Ultimate Cooking Experience"!

Light It Up!

Before lighting up your EGG, you want to make sure that you always use high-quality lump charcoal. My preferred charcoal of choice is Big Green Egg Oak & Hickory Natural Lump Charcoal. It is made in the USA from ultra-premium hardwood and contains NO additives, fillers, or nitrates. All of this essentially ensures that the food will taste amazing when cooked on the EGG. If the EGG is empty and clean, fill the EGG to the top of the firebox with charcoal from the bag.

If there is leftover ash and charcoal from your previous cooks, make sure to remove the cooking grid, stir the old charcoals, and use the ash tools to remove ashes from the EGG.

The rule of thumb is to clean your EGG ONLY when it's completely cool. The EGG gets very hot and stays hot even after you're finished EGGin'. So safety first! I would suggest cleaning your cooking grid with a bristle-free wire grill brush after every cook, and cleaning out and removing the ash from the EGG after every few cooks. This will ensure proper air flow and keep the EGG always operating at full capacity. A clean EGG is a happy EGG.

NEVER, under any circumstances, use liquid lighter fluid to light your EGG. The chemicals and additives will penetrate and remain in the porous ceramic food chamber. Not to mention it would contaminate the flavor and smell of the food you're EGGin'. So just don't do it, please. The Big Green Egg natural charcoal starters are your best friend when it comes to lighting the EGG. Break a couple starters in half, light them, and place them in the charcoal. The Big Green Egg EGGniter charcoal starters are also great ways to start the fire on an EGG; both butane and electric versions are available. Just step away from the lighter fluid . . . You've been warned.

When trying to reach my optimal cooking temperature, I start out by leaving the top vent and the bottom vent completely wide open for the first 15 minutes. As the EGG begins to heat up, I close the top and bottom vents halfway as I gradually work toward my desired cooking temperature.

A couple things to take note of: the EGG is a BIG ceramic smoker, so it takes a little time and patience to warm up . . . but it will all be worth it when it does. Also, when adjusting the EGG to your desired temperature, begin to slightly close the vent when you get within 5 degrees of that temperature. That will keep the temperature constant and steady throughout the cook as long as the lid is closed. If you're 5 degrees below or above your desired cook temperature, no need to pull your hair out; it'll be all right! The EGG Genius is a handy device that controls the EGG temperature automatically. The EGG Genius mounts to the bottom vent of the EGG and uses a tiny fan and probe to give you the exact temperature you want. (Pretty cool, right?!) Whenever you're done EGGin' on the Big Green Egg, close all of the vents and allow the EGG to cool completely. This process should take several hours, and larger EGGs take longer to cool down.

Mind Your Eyebrows and Burp . . .

Throughout your cook on the EGG, you will probably need to open the EGG for several reasons. Removing meat from the grill, saucing your ribs, flipping your chicken, etc. . . . Whatever the reason is, make sure to always "burp" your EGG when you open it. "Burping" your EGG means you open your EGG partially (about 2 to 4 inches), and pause before raising the dome completely. This allows air to slowly and safely enter the dome, preventing any flare-ups that could escape from the front toward you. So mind your eyebrows and burp the EGG!

Direct Grilling

Direct grilling is pretty straightforward on the EGG. Fill the EGG to the top of the firebox with charcoal and bring the EGG to your desired temperature. Direct grilling is great for high-heat cooking and getting a nice hard sear on steaks and chops. Be careful not to walk away and keep the lid open; this can cause potential flare-ups and (spoiler alert) burned food.

Indirect Cooking

For indirect cooking on the EGG, you add the convEGGtor to the EGG. This essentially converts the EGG into a convection oven by circulating hot air throughout the EGG and

around the food, cooking it through with a very even heat. Outside of using this primary setup for smoking and roasting, indirect cooking is great for baking cookies, pies, cakes, and any baked goods in the EGG. For indirect cooking, fill the EGG to the top of the firebox with charcoal; if you plan on using wood chips or wood chunks, feel free to add them at this point. Light the EGG, as instructed before, and place the convEGGtor in the EGG once the fire is lit. Adding a drip pan on top of the convEGGtor will catch any fat, oil, or sauce that may cause any flare-ups while roasting and smoking.

Meat Doneness

Cooking times are only a template and not an exact science. Meat size, meat temperature, the weather outside, the wind, how much charcoal you have in the EGG, and so on, are all variables that factor into your cooking times and meat doneness. Sight, touch, and a great digital meat thermometer will be the tools you need to accurately know when your meat is done. With time will come experience, and with experience comes knowledge.

For steaks, roasts, and poultry, it's good to know that they will continue to cook after they're removed from the grill. This is called "carryover cooking" and will cause the internal temperature of the food to rise 5 to 10 degrees more when it's "resting." So it's imperative to cook the protein 5 degrees below your desired internal temperature, to avoid overcooking your food.

Knowing Your Meats

Know your meats and their ideal cooking temperatures.

Beef steaks and large beef roasts (rare doneness)	120°F
Beef steaks and large beef roasts (medium-rare doneness)	125°F
Beef brisket	200°F
Ground beef (medium doneness)	160°F
Pork chops and pork tenderloins (medium doneness)	145 to 150°F
Pork butt (shoulder)/pulled pork	200°F
Chicken breast	165°F
Chicken thighs, legs, and wings	180°F
Duck drumettes	165°F
Lamb chops (medium-rare)	135°F
Ground lamb burgers	160°F

Beef Temperature Chart

Rare: 120°F to 125°F
Red cool center; texture is tender and soft.

Medium-rare: 130°F to 135°F
Red warm center; texture is slightly firm.

Medium: 140°F to 145°F
Hot pink center; texture is slightly firmer.

Medium-well: 150°F to 155°F
Mostly brown center, with a thin line of pink; texture is firm.

Well done: 160°F +
Completely brown; texture is very dry.

The EGGin' Culinary Arsenal

Here are the tools and equipment I always use while I'm EGGin'! The EGG speaks for itself and is the most important tool of them all. But I feel like having the right tools in your culinary arsenal gives you exactly what you need to have the perfect cook on your EGG. So let's jump right into it . . .

Sharp Knife

As a chef I find a sharp, high-quality chef's knife to be my most important tool in the kitchen and while cooking. It slices, it carves, it chops, it trims, and it helps you fabricate your product. Nothing in the kitchen can substitute for a sharp chef's knife . . . Well, except for an even sharper knife! A sharp boning knife is perfect for removing the silver skin, excess hard fat, and unwanted bones from large roasts, briskets, and pork shoulders.

Big Green Egg Digital Thermometer

The Big Green Egg digital thermometer eliminates all of the guesswork of knowing the temperature of your steaks, chicken, chops, and roasts. It gives a fast and precise temperature read every time.

KitchenAid 7-Cup Food Processor

This is the perfect tool to blend sauces and salsas and chop vegetables if you're ever in a crunch for time.

Black Nitrile Gloves

Whenever you need to get down and dirty, a pair of these will help get the job done. Whether it's rubbing down or marinating large, beautiful pieces of meat, handling charcoal, or cleaning your EGG, keep your own mitts clean and pristine with some black nitrile gloves.

The Big Green Egg Carbon Steel Wok

The Big Green Egg carbon steel wok is perfect for quick stir-fries, fried rice, and lo mein and can whip up perfectly cooked vegetables that are still crunchy and delicious in minutes. This baby is one of my favorite things in my EGGin' culinary arsenal!

The Big Green Egg EGG Genius

The EGG Genius is the one-stop shop for all your EGG temperature control needs. It's a no-brainer for temperature control.

Big Green Egg Cast-Iron Skillets and Saucepot

Big Green Egg cast-iron pans are great for getting a nice hard sear on steaks and chops on the EGG; they're perfect for butter basting as well. Whenever I discuss sautéing and cooking sauces in *EGGin'*, all the pans and pots I use are cast-iron. They're heavy-duty and heat resistant enough to handle the heat of the EGG. The saucepot is great for cooking sauces, reheating sauces, and keeping sauces warm on the EGG.

Big Green Egg Silicone BBQ Mitts

Whenever you gotta grab something hot, make sure you slip these on first! They withstand temperatures up to 450°F.

Big Green Egg Silicone-Tipped Tongs

I have a pair of these silicone-tipped tongs in both 16-inch and 12-inch versions. Whenever I have to flip or take anything off the EGG, I always have a pair of these within reach. The nonslip tongs grab and hold your food securely and are heat resistant up to 500°F. You, my friend, Mr. Tongs, have job security as long as I'm around!

Big Green Egg Cedar Grilling Planks

These planks were made for EGGin', and that's just what they'll do . . . These cedar planks are the perfect solution for cooking fish and seafood through, while still retaining all of their glorious moisture and also imparting a mild, fragrant smoky flavor.

Disposable Aluminum Foil Pans

Perfect to season in, cook, hold food, use as drip pans . . . and they can be used as to-go containers for those exceptionally hungry guests! Dirty 'em up, burn 'em, mess 'em up, then just toss 'em in the garbage when you're done. I buy these in bulk.

Big Green Egg Solid Teak Cutting Boards

I prefer to use these solid teak cutting boards because they're made with high-quality wood, they're heavy-duty, and they last a long time, as long as you take good care of them. I've thrown everything I could at these cutting boards, but they still last the test of time.

Big Green Egg Perforated Grids

I use the perforated grids for delicate proteins such as flaky fish and seafood, as well as for smaller vegetables. They prevent the food from falling into your EGG. So the food goes into your mouth . . . where it belongs!

Pink Butcher Paper

I always make sure to keep plenty of pink butcher paper on hand. The butcher paper allows the meat to retain moisture and breathe a little more, without steaming it when the meat is wrapped. Whenever I double-wrap my ribs, briskets, and pork shoulder, I always use pink butcher paper.

Big Green Egg Natural Lump Charcoal

This is my go-to charcoal: high-quality USA natural hickory and oak lump charcoal. It works 100 percent of the time, ALL the time!

Wood and Me

The selection of wood chips and wood chunks you use to smoke with on the EGG is also a very important ingredient in the recipe. Feel free to experiment by mixing and matching different wood chips to create your own flavor profiles. To use wood chips in your EGG, once the charcoal is lit and the EGG is at your desired temperature, spread the wood chips evenly on top of the charcoal.

Apple: Apple wood has a light, mild, and natural sweetness. It's great for all poultry, seafood, pork, and beef, as well as desserts, for nice light smoke flavor.

Cherry: Cherry wood is lightly fruity and mild. It's perfect for poultry, beef, lamb, and pork.

Pecan: Pecan wood has a rich, sweet, mellow, and slightly nutty flavor. Poultry, beef, and pork can all get down with these delicate flavors. This wood is a must with my Bourbon–Ginger Pecan Pie (page 134).

Hickory: Hickory wood has a very savory and sweet-bold "bacony"-like taste to it. Obviously, it's great with pork and also red meat. A lot of Southern-style barbecue utilizes hickory wood.

Pimento: Pimento wood is spicy, sweet, and very floral and has flavors of allspice. It is essential in smoking my truly authentic Jamaican Jerk Chicken with Pineapple-Habanero Sauce (page 60).

Maple: Maple wood is subtle and mild. The sweet notes of the maple make it perfect for poultry and pork.

Don't Be Salty

I prefer to use Morton's Coarse Kosher Salt and coarse-grind black pepper for red meats, pork, and poultry. They give me a visual cue when I season my meat and provide great texture to the meat as well. Whenever I'm slicing or carving a large steak or roast, I like to sometimes finish it with Maldon Sea Salt Flakes. These are soft and crunchy sea salt flakes that provide a fresh minerality and clean taste to help enhance the dish. For seafood, I prefer to use a white ground pepper, or a fine-grind black pepper, so it doesn't overpower the protein.

Let's Get EGGin'

EGGin' is a look inside my personal playbook and contains the food that molded me into the chef and lover of barbecue I am today. These recipes signify who I am, the food I grew up with, my culinary training, close to ten years of EGGin' on the Big Green Egg, more than thirty years of grilling experience, and food that I just find downright delicious. They're comforting, they're international, they're flavorful, they're soulful, and they all taste great coming off the EGG. These are recipes from the heart, and they are a very clear reflection of the food that makes me happy.

When I started constructing the *EGGin'* cookbook, I wanted to share my love of food with the world. I wanted to show the simplicity in cooking delicious food. So many times, people are intimidated by cooking because of their lack of knowledge, and some folks are just downright afraid to cook. But that's all right, and that's okay, because this cookbook is going to take your hand and walk you to the promised land. It contains simple and easy-to-follow recipes that will impress not only yourself but also your guests. My aim is to empower you with the tools and culinary know-how to open that EGG up with confidence and be able to smoke and grill with the best of them. The recipes and techniques are interchangeable and can be applied to several applications with different meats, poultry, vegetables, and spirits.

EGGin' is a celebration of life, love, family, friends, and great times! Great food can help make a bad day a great day and turn a frown upside down. As you flip through the pages and grill, smoke, barbecue, cook, bake, and shake and stir cocktails, I hope that you learn and pick up some great tips, tricks, and tasty techniques along the way. I literally LOVE food—all types of food—and I hope you will, too, after cooking some of my recipes. *EGGin'* is a party, so get ready to eat till you grow a pants size or two and get happy!

CHAPTER

2

FIRST ACTS

(APPS, SOUP, SALADS)

Every headliner needs a great opening act . . . That FIRST ACT is always going to set the tempo and precedence of what's to come next. And that's exactly what the first course does. A great appetizer will always put your best foot forward and prime the appetites of your guests with the promise and allure of more delicious things to come in the meal. A not-so-great appetizer . . . Meh . . . Not so much. Small plates, soups, salads, and sharable plates, this chapter has everything you need to set up an intimate meal or a large gathering for success. And just so you know, we're starting out strong . . . with BIG, BOLD flavors from beginning to end. Okay . . . That's enough talking . . . Let's get EGGin'!

Hoisin Barbecue Duck Drumettes

Makes 10 to 12 servings

Growing up in New Jersey and the surrounding tristate area, great Chinese food restaurants were not lacking. A lot of the foods I tasted and enjoyed growing up served as my culinary road map in my career as well. Hoisin is a thick and wildly flavorful sauce, often used as a glaze in Chinese cooking, which makes it perfect for this barbecue sauce with grilled duck drumettes. Watch out, chicken wings— you got some competition!

3 pounds duck drumettes

RUB
2 tablespoons kosher salt

1 tablespoon black pepper

1 teaspoon smoked paprika

1 teaspoon Chinese five spice

1 teaspoon granulated garlic

½ teaspoon granulated onion

1 teaspoon dark brown sugar

SAUCE
1 cup ketchup

7 ounces hoisin sauce

1 tablespoon peeled and
    freshly grated ginger root

2 cloves garlic, minced

3 tablespoons rice wine vinegar

1 teaspoon sriracha

2 tablespoons honey

½ teaspoon soy sauce

Prepare the EGG to cook direct at 350°F. Rinse and pat the duck drumettes dry. To make the rub, place all of the ingredients in a small bowl and mix until well incorporated. Season the drumettes with the rub and line them around the outer perimeter of the EGG cooking grid. Grill drumettes on one side for 15 minutes, and then grill on the other side for 15 minutes, or until cooked through and the duck fat has rendered.

While the drumettes are grilling, make the sauce. Place a medium cast-iron saucepot in the middle of the EGG cooking grid and add all of the ingredients. Bring the mixture to a boil and continue to cook for 4 to 5 minutes, until it reaches a sauce-like consistency. Remove the pot from the EGG and cool the sauce to room temperature.

Once the drumettes are crispy and golden brown, glaze them with the sauce until they are sticky and lacquered. Remove them from the EGG and serve right away.

Thai Green Curry Chicken Wings

Makes 4 to 6 servings

I'm all about a little spice in my life! The flavors in Thai green curry are lemongrass, chili, kaffir lime, coriander, and shrimp paste. Any day I can enjoy a good curry, is a good day! The curry sauce is balanced with the creamy notes and natural sweetness from the coconut milk. It's the perfect mix of spice and sweet. So get ready to transport your taste buds to Southeast Asia.

2 pounds chicken wings,
   drums and flats separate

RUB

2 teaspoons kosher salt

1 teaspoon black pepper

1 teaspoon white pepper

1 teaspoon smoked paprika

1 teaspoon granulated garlic

1 teaspoon granulated onion

1 teaspoon yellow curry powder

SAUCE

2 tablespoons olive oil

1 tablespoon minced fresh lemongrass

3 cloves garlic, minced

¼ cup minced yellow onion

1½ tablespoons Thai green curry paste

1 (13.66-ounce) can coconut milk (full fat)

1 tablespoon granulated sugar
   (for a sweeter sauce, add an additional
   teaspoon of sugar)

Kosher salt and black pepper

¼ cup chopped fresh cilantro, for garnish

Prepare the EGG to cook direct at 375°F. Rinse and pat the chicken wings dry. To make the rub, place all of the ingredients in a small bowl and whisk until well incorporated. Season the wings with the rub and allow them to come to room temperature for 15 to 20 minutes.

Meanwhile, to make the sauce, place a medium cast-iron saucepot on the EGG cooking grid and add the olive oil, lemongrass, garlic, and onion and sauté for about 1 minute, or until fragrant. Stir in the curry paste and sauté for an additional 90 seconds, then add the coconut milk and sugar. Bring the sauce to a boil and continue to cook for 8 to 10 minutes, until thickened to a sauce-like consistency. Season to taste with salt and pepper. Divide the sauce into two bowls: one is for tossing the wings, and the other will be used for dipping sauce.

Lay the wings around the outer perimeter of the EGG cooking grid and grill them for 14 to 16 minutes on each side, until golden brown and cooked to 165°F. Remove the wings from the EGG and toss them with half of the sauce. Place the tossed wings back on the EGG for 1 minute on each side. Remove the wings from the EGG and toss again with the sauce. Place the twice-coated wings back on the EGG for 1 minute on each side. Remove the wings from the EGG and garnish with the cilantro. Serve the wings with the remaining sauce.

Ancho-Grilled Flank Steak with Mango Salad

Makes 4 to 6 servings

I've got a soft spot for Mexican spices, and I look no further than ancho chiles to provide that perfect amount of smoky-sweet heat. These dried poblano peppers make for an exceptional rub, especially when it comes to red meat—the intense beef flavor of flank steak pairs very well with the ancho rub. The sliced mangos and mango vinaigrette add contrast in taste, texture, and temperature and help to cool down the spice in the ancho. The feta cheese lends a nice creamy note as well. This salad hits on all cylinders!

2 pounds flank steak

RUB

1 tablespoon ancho chile powder

½ teaspoon ground cumin

½ teaspoon granulated garlic

2 tablespoons kosher salt

1 teaspoon black pepper

VINAIGRETTE

½ cup mango nectar

2 tablespoons honey

½ cup olive oil

1 tablespoon honey

3 tablespoons rice wine vinegar

1 tablespoon Dijon mustard

Kosher salt and black pepper

¼ teaspoon crushed red pepper

SALAD

24 ounces baby kale spring mix

1 large mango, thinly sliced lengthwise, divided

¼ red onion, thinly sliced, divided

4 ounces crumbled feta cheese or goat cheese, divided

Kosher salt and black pepper

(continued)

(continued from page 16)

Prepare the EGG to cook direct at 450°F. Pat the flank steak dry on both sides. To make the rub, place all of the ingredients in a small bowl and mix until well incorporated. Liberally season the steak with the rub on both sides and allow it to come to room temperature for about 30 minutes.

While the meat is resting, make the vinaigrette. Combine all of the ingredients in a medium bowl and whisk together until well incorporated. Season to taste with salt and pepper. Set aside.

Grill the steak on the EGG cooking grid for 4 to 5 minutes per side for perfect medium-rare (or to desired doneness). The flank steak should be nice and browned. Remove the steak from the EGG and allow it to rest on a cutting board for about 8 minutes. Slice the steak into ½-inch slices on the bias, against the grain.

To make the salad, place the greens in a large bowl. Add half of the sliced mango, half of the sliced red onion, half of the feta cheese, and salt and pepper to taste and drizzle with the vinaigrette. Toss the salad and garnish with the remaining mango, onion, and feta cheese. Finish with 4 to 5 slices of steak on each salad plate.

Smoked Wings with Alabama White Barbecue Sauce

Makes 6 to 8 servings

The chicken wing remains a constant go-to and staple on the EGG . . . and any backyard barbecue, for that matter. Brining the wings in salt, sugar, herbs, and aromatics overnight allows the flavors to penetrate deeper into the wings. This process provides great flavor and keeps the chicken moist while smoking on the EGG. The Alabama white sauce complements the wings perfectly with the nice and creamy spice from the Japanese Kewpie mayo and horseradish. Get ready to put this wing recipe in your EGGin' arsenal.

2 pounds chicken wings,
   drums and flats separated

BRINE

2 cups water

¼ cup kosher salt

1 cup packed dark brown sugar

2 cloves garlic, smashed

1 fresh thyme sprig

SAUCE

1 cup Kewpie mayo

¼ cup apple cider vinegar

1 tablespoon honey

1 tablespoon Dijon mustard

½ teaspoon hot sauce

1 teaspoon Worcestershire sauce

1 tablespoon prepared horseradish

½ teaspoon granulated garlic

½ teaspoon granulated onion

½ teaspoon white pepper

¼ teaspoon cayenne pepper

½ teaspoon smoked paprika

Kosher salt and black pepper

1 cup apple wood chips, soaked for 1 hour in 2 cups water

Rinse the chicken wings and pat dry. To make the brine, place all of the ingredients in a medium cast-iron saucepot on the stove and bring to a boil. Once boiling, remove the pot from the heat and cool the brine to room temperature. Add the wings and the brine to a large resealable plastic bag and refrigerate overnight, or for at least 4 hours.

To make the sauce, add all of the ingredients to a medium bowl and whisk until well incorporated. Season to taste with salt and pepper. Set aside.

Prepare the EGG to cook direct at 400°F. Remove the wings from the brine and pat dry. Drain the wood chips and place them in the EGG over the hot coals. Once the EGG is smoking, lay the wings on the outer perimeter of the cooking grid and grill for 14 to 16 minutes per side, until they are crispy, golden brown, and cooked through. Toss the wings in half of the sauce and serve the remaining sauce on the side.

Grilled Watermelon Salad with Tequila-Lime Vinaigrette

Makes 4 servings

What screams summer more than a perfectly ripe, sweet watermelon? It's refreshing, bright, and just what the doctor ordered on a hot and humid summer day. This salad ups the ante with chargrilled watermelon. This method caramelizes and intensifies the sugars while also giving it a nice smoky note. The saltiness of the Mexican cotija cheese mixed with the spice of the Tajín and the splash of tequila provides just the right kick the vinaigrette needs. This is one of my go-to summer salads!

½ medium seedless watermelon, cut into 1-inch slices (rind removed)

VINAIGRETTE

1 ounce reposado tequila

1 ounce agave nectar

Juice from ½ lime

1 tablespoon Dijon mustard

2 tablespoons apple cider vinegar

1 teaspoon honey

2 tablespoons chopped fresh cilantro

Kosher salt and black pepper

SALAD

12 to 15 mint leaves

¼ red onion, thinly sliced

4 ounces crumbled cotija cheese

Tajín classic seasoning

Kosher salt and black pepper

Prepare the EGG to cook direct at 450°F. Grill the watermelon slices on the EGG cooking grid for about 5 minutes per side, or until they develop nice charred grill marks on both sides. Remove the watermelon slices from the EGG and place them on a platter.

To make the vinaigrette, place all of the ingredients in a medium bowl and whisk until fully incorporated. Season to taste with salt and pepper. Set aside.

To assemble the salad, scatter the mint and red onion over the watermelon, drizzle the vinaigrette all over, and top with the cheese. Season to taste with Tajín and salt and pepper.

Grilled Shrimp and Pear Salad with Calabrian Vinaigrette

Makes 3 to 4 servings

You had me at shrimp! This very flavorful and festive salad is perfect for grilling season . . . or anytime, really. The smoky notes of the paprika really shine with the grilled shrimp. I absolutely love to combine savory notes with sweet, and this salad is no exception. Tossing the pears with olive oil and honey lends a nice earthy and satisfying flavor to the salad. And the focaccia croutons?! C'mon . . . yes, yes, and yes! Combine all of that with the zesty spice of the Calabrian vinaigrette and we have a winner-winner shrimp and pear salad dinner.

CROUTONS

3 tablespoons olive oil

2 slices focaccia bread, diced into crouton size

Pinch of kosher salt and black pepper

VINAIGRETTE

6 finely minced Calabrian chiles

½ cup olive oil

¼ cup sherry vinegar

2 tablespoons honey

Kosher salt and black pepper

PEARS

2 medium Bartlett pears, seeded and sliced into ½-inch slices

2 teaspoons honey

2 tablespoons olive oil

SHRIMP

1 pound shrimp (12/16 count)

1 tablespoon kosher salt

2 teaspoons black pepper

1 teaspoon smoked paprika

2 tablespoons olive oil

SALAD

12 ounces arugula

3 ounces goat cheese, divided

Kosher salt and black pepper

(continued)

(continued from page 22)

Prepare the EGG to cook direct at 400°F. To make the croutons, place a cast-iron pan on the EGG cooking grid and add the olive oil. Add the focaccia and season with a pinch of salt and pepper. Toast the focaccia on all sides for 4 to 6 minutes, until golden brown. Once the croutons are toasty, remove the pan from the EGG and set aside.

To make the vinaigrette, combine all of the ingredients in a small bowl and whisk until well incorporated. Season to taste with salt and pepper. Set aside.

To make the pears, toss them with the honey and olive oil. Grill them on the EGG cooking grid for about 2 minutes per side, or until the pears have grill marks on each side.

To make the shrimp, add the spices, olive oil, and shrimp to a small bowl. Soak 6 to 8 wooden skewers in water for at least 30 minutes and use 2 parallel skewers to double-skewer the shrimp. Grill on the EGG cooking grid for 3 to 4 minutes per side, until golden brown and cooked through.

To assemble the salad, toss the arugula with half of the goat cheese and half of the focaccia croutons, then lightly dress with the vinaigrette and a pinch of salt and pepper, and toss again. Divide the salad among three or four salad plates or serve on one big platter. Finish the plates by dividing the pears, shrimp, and remaining goat cheese and croutons among the salad plates or evenly distribute over the large platter.

Chorizo-Arugula Salad with Parmesan and Chorizo Vinaigrette

Makes 4 to 6 servings

This salad hits a lot of different flavor notes and doesn't disappoint. The spiciness from the dried chorizo is balanced by the sweetness from the orange juice and honey, while the peppery arugula is perfectly complemented by the creamy Parmesan and the fresh pop of the cherry tomatoes. This is the perfect salad to accompany any meal.

VINAIGRETTE

1 tablespoon olive oil

7 ounces dried chorizo, small diced

1 cup bottled orange juice

1 tablespoon Dijon mustard

2 tablespoons sherry vinegar

1 tablespoon honey

⅓ cup olive oil

Kosher salt and black pepper

¼ teaspoon crushed red pepper

SALAD

8 to 12 ounces baby arugula
(about 2 ounces per serving)

¼ pound cherry tomatoes, halved

2 ounces freshly grated
Parmesan cheese

2 ounces Parmesan cheese,
freshly peeled in ribbons with
a vegetable peeler

Kosher salt and black pepper

Prepare the EGG to cook direct at 400°F. To make the vinaigrette, place a medium cast-iron saucepot on the EGG cooking grid and add the olive oil. Add the chorizo and sauté for about 5 minutes, or until it is crisp and the fat has rendered. Remove the cooked chorizo from the oil and set aside. Pour the remaining oil from the saucepot into a medium bowl and set aside.

Place a small cast-iron saucepot on the EGG cooking grid and add the orange juice. Cook for about 6 minutes, or until reduced to one-third of its original volume. Once reduced, measure ⅓ cup of the orange juice and add to the bowl with the chorizo oil. Add the mustard, vinegar, honey, olive oil, pinch of salt and black pepper, and crushed red pepper and whisk until well incorporated.

To make the salad, add the arugula, chorizo, and tomatoes to a large bowl. Drizzle the salad with the desired amount of vinaigrette and lightly toss. To finish, sprinkle the salad with the grated Parmesan, Parmesan ribbons, and pinch of salt and pepper to taste.

Grilled Broccoli Caesar

Makes 8 servings

Caesar dressing is a really tasty and simple way to add a burst of flavor to any salad or vegetable. There's a reason it's on almost every restaurant's menu—it just tastes really good! This easy dressing adds salt, acidity, and the highly coveted cheese factor to anything it dresses up. Grilling vegetables unlocks a lot of great flavors as they caramelize. It's the perfect way to get kids and picky eaters to indulge in their vegetables. Feel free to add as much freshly grated Parmesan as humanly possible to the grilled broccoli . . . It will be our little secret . . . maybe.

DRESSING

1 teaspoon minced fresh garlic

1 teaspoon anchovy paste

1 tablespoon freshly squeezed lemon juice

1 teaspoon Dijon mustard

1 teaspoon Worcestershire sauce

1 cup mayonnaise

½ cup freshly grated Parmesan or Pecorino cheese

2 dashes of hot sauce

Kosher salt and black pepper

BROCCOLI

½ cup olive oil

4 cloves garlic, minced

2 heads broccoli, quartered and blanched in salted water for 90 seconds

Pinch of kosher salt and black pepper

2 ounces Parmesan cheese wedge, freshly shaved ribbons

Prepare the EGG to cook direct at 400°F. To make the dressing, place all of the ingredients in a medium bowl and whisk until well incorporated. Season to taste with salt and pepper. Set aside.

To make the broccoli, whisk the olive oil and garlic together in a small bowl and then drizzle over the broccoli. Season it with salt and pepper and place directly on the EGG cooking grid. Grill the broccoli for 4 to 5 minutes per side, until slightly charred and browned. Remove the broccoli from the EGG and drizzle with the dressing. To make the cheese ribbons, use a vegetable peeler to peel the cheese wedge. Finish with Parmesan cheese ribbons.

Crab Parmesan–Spinach Dip

Makes 6 to 8 servings

Tailgate parties, birthdays, family dinners, or even solo movie date nights for a party of one—any time is the perfect time for this delicious, piping hot spinach and cheese dip! But this isn't just any ordinary dip; the sweet and briny notes from the luscious lump crabmeat pair perfectly with the sharp and creamy mix of Parmesan and mozzarella. Grab the chips and let's dip.

3 tablespoons olive oil

6 ounces baby portobella (or crimini) mushrooms, thinly sliced

6 ounces fresh spinach

3 cloves garlic, minced

Kosher salt and black pepper

¼ teaspoon crushed red pepper

2 tablespoons unsalted butter

2 tablespoons all-purpose flour

2 cups whole milk

1 cup heavy cream

4 ounces shredded mozzarella cheese

6 ounces freshly shredded Parmesan cheese, divided

1 teaspoon granulated garlic

1 teaspoon granulated onion

8 ounces lump crabmeat

Tortilla chips, grilled pita bread, or veggies (carrots, celery, red bell pepper), for serving

Prepare the EGG to cook direct at 400°F. Place a 9-inch cast-iron pan on the EGG cooking grid and add the olive oil. Add the mushrooms and sauté for 4 to 5 minutes, until tender. Add the spinach, garlic, a pinch of salt and black pepper, and crushed red pepper and sauté for about 1 minute, or until the spinach is wilted and tender. Remove the spinach and mushrooms from the pan and set them aside. In the same pan, melt the butter and whisk in the flour for 2 to 3 minutes, until it makes a roux. Add the milk and heavy cream and bring to a boil while continuously whisking, until the sauce is slightly thickened.

Add the mozzarella, 3 ounces of the Parmesan, and the granulated garlic and granulated onion and whisk until melted and a cheese sauce forms. Fold in the crabmeat and sautéed spinach and mushrooms. Season to taste with salt and pepper. Remove the pan from the EGG and top the dip with the remaining 3 ounces Parmesan. Broil the top of the dip with a torch until golden brown. Allow the dip to cool for 6 to 8 minutes before eating. Serve with tortilla chips, grilled pita bread, or veggies.

Pulled Pork Egg Rolls

Makes 8 to 10 servings

So you just smoked a glorious pork butt on the EGG, and it was delightful. "What to do with all that leftover pork butt?" Four words . . . pulled pork egg rolls. Far East–meets–West when you stuff flaky fried egg rolls with the pulled pork and wok-fried vegetables. I highly recommend serving these with Sriracha–Honey Barbecue Sauce (page 59) as well as a cold beer!

FILLING

3 tablespoons vegetable oil

1 pound Sweet and Spicy Pulled Pork
  (page 74)

½ teaspoon sesame oil

½ medium yellow onion, small diced

2 green onions, green and white parts
  minced

3 cloves garlic, minced

2 cups shredded Napa cabbage

1 cup shredded carrots

Pinch of kosher salt and black pepper

1 teaspoon granulated garlic

1 teaspoon granulated onion

1 teaspoon smoked paprika

EGG ROLLS

8 to 10 (7 by 7-inch) egg roll wrappers

2 medium eggs

½ cup water

3 cups vegetable oil, for frying

Sriracha–Honey Barbecue Sauce
  (page 59), for serving

Prepare the EGG to cook direct with a wok setup at 400°F. To make the filling, add the vegetable oil to the wok. Add the pulled pork and stir-fry for 2 to 3 minutes, until heated, browned, and lightly crispy. Remove the pork from the wok and set aside in a small bowl.

Add the sesame oil to the wok and immediately stir-fry the yellow onions, green onions, and garlic for about 2 minutes, or until fragrant. Add the cabbage, carrots, salt and pepper, granulated garlic, granulated onion, and paprika. Stir-fry for 4 to 5 minutes, until the cabbage is tender. Add the pork back to the wok and stir-fry until well incorporated and warmed. Season to taste with salt and pepper. Allow the filling to cool to room temperature.

To assemble the egg rolls, lay out the wrapper in the shape of a diamond, so one of the pointed ends is facing you. Place about 3 heaping tablespoons of the pork filling in the middle of each wrapper. In a small bowl, whisk together the eggs and the water. Brush all four sides of the wrapper with the egg wash. Fold the bottom corner over the filling, rolling only halfway to snugly cover the filling. Fold in the left and right sides across the filling, brush the top of the egg roll once more with the egg wash, then finish rolling to the top corner.

Place the oil in the wok and bring it up to 350°F to 375°F, until it begins to shimmer. Carefully fry the egg rolls in batches of 2 at a time for 2 to 3 minutes, until golden brown. Remove the egg rolls with a slotted spoon and lay them on a paper towel–lined sheet pan to drain. Serve them warm with the barbeque sauce.

Chinatown Oysters Rockefeller

Makes 4 servings

I bet you can't just eat one of these delectable oysters. Oysters Rockefeller is traditionally served with Parmesan, bread crumbs, and spinach, which is a delicious combo in itself. However, this recipe serves as an homage to my late nights in Chinatown in NYC as a teenager and the many mini food tours I took after-hours. The inclusion of the sweet Chinese sausage, the bitter-peppery yu choy Chinese greens, the umami of the Kewpie mayo, and the fresh lump crabmeat elevates the oysters to heavenly bliss. (Drool . . .)

STUFFING

4 Chinese-style sweet sausage links
 (about 8 ounces)

16 yu choy leaves

1 clove garlic, minced

Pinch of kosher salt

1 tablespoon olive oil

½ cup Kewpie mayo

2 teaspoons Tia Chieu Chili Sa-té paste

1 teaspoon sriracha

½ teaspoon Worcestershire sauce

Juice of ½ small sour orange
 (such as Seville)

Kosher salt and black pepper

½ pound jumbo lump crabmeat

½ cup panko (Japanese bread crumbs)

12 large gulf oysters, cleaned, scrubbed,
 and shucked

¼ cup chopped fresh cilantro,
 for garnish

Prepare the EGG to cook direct at 375°F. To make the stuffing, place the sausage on the EGG cooking grid and grill for 8 to 10 minutes, until lightly charred and cooked through and the internal temperature reaches 165°F. Remove the sausage from the EGG and allow it to cool for about 5 minutes. Then mince the sausage and set aside.

In a small bowl, add the yu choy, garlic, salt, and olive oil and toss well until coated. Lay the yu choy on the EGG cooking grid and grill for 30 to 45 seconds on each side, until the leaves wilt and slightly char. Remove them from the grill, rough chop, and set aside.

In a medium bowl, combine the mayo, chili-garlic paste, sriracha, Worcestershire sauce, sour orange juice, and a pinch of salt and pepper and whisk until well incorporated. Add the lump crabmeat, the chopped yu choy, half of the sausage, and the panko. Fold until well incorporated and season to taste with salt and pepper.

Prepare the EGG to cook direct at 425°F. Place about 2 tablespoons of crab stuffing inside each oyster. Place the oysters on the EGG cooking grid and cook for 8 to 10 minutes, until the crabmeat stuffing is golden brown and the oysters are sizzling. Remove the oysters from the EGG and serve hot immediately, garnished with the remaining half of the sausage and the cilantro.

Barbecue Pork Belly Burnt End Nachos with Pepper Jack Cheese Sauce

Makes 6 to 8 servings

There are few things in life that are as rewarding as a plate of messy, guilty-pleasure nachos with toppings of cheese, meat, and fixin's piled over warm, crispy corn tortilla chips. If you're just like me, you may have asked yourself this same question many times: "If the cheese sticks to multiple nachos when you lift one up, is that considered one nacho?" Let me put your mind at ease, "Yes, it's one nacho . . . It's all scientific and not up for debate!" This combination of sticky smoked pork belly glazed to perfection with rum barbecue sauce and pepper jack cheese sauce pretty much speaks for itself. And it's saying "Eat me!"

1 cup cherry wood chips, soaked for at least 1 hour in 2 cups water

PORK

3 pounds pork belly, cleaned and trimmed

Apple juice, for spritzing

3 tablespoons honey

RUB

2 tablespoons kosher salt

2 tablespoons black pepper

2 tablespoons brown sugar

2 tablespoons granulated sugar

2 teaspoons smoked paprika

1 teaspoon granulated garlic

1 teaspoon granulated onion

½ teaspoon cayenne pepper

BARBECUE SAUCE

½ cup spiced dark rum

18 ounces of your favorite barbecue sauce or one of the barbecue sauces in this cookbook

CHEESE SAUCE

1 tablespoon unsalted butter

1 tablespoon all-purpose flour

1 pint heavy cream

¼ teaspoon salt

¼ teaspoon black pepper

¼ teaspoon cayenne pepper

¼ teaspoon granulated garlic

¼ teaspoon granulated onion

1½ cups shredded pepper jack cheese

Tortilla chips, for serving

(continued)

(continued from page 32)

Prepare the EGG to cook indirect with a drip pan at 275°F. Drain the wood chips and place them in the EGG over the hot coals. To make the pork, rinse the pork belly, pat dry, and cut into 1-inch cubes. To make the rub, place all of the ingredients in a small bowl and mix thoroughly. Season the pork belly generously with the rub on all sides. Put a wire rack on a half sheet pan and place the pork belly cubes on the rack, leaving space between each cube. Put the pan on the EGG cooking grid and smoke for 3 hours, spritzing the pork belly with apple juice every hour.

Meanwhile, to make the barbecue sauce, on the stovetop, in a small saucepot add the rum and carefully bring to a boil. Cook until reduced by one-third of its original volume and then add the barbecue sauce. Bring to a boil and continue to cook for 3 to 4 minutes.

Remove the pork belly from the wire rack and place directly into an aluminum half pan. Add about three-quarters of the barbecue sauce to the pork belly, along with the honey. Toss to completely coat. Cover the pan with aluminum foil and cook on the EGG cooking grid for an additional hour, until the pork belly is sticky, well lacquered, and fork tender.

Prepare the EGG to cook direct at 400°F. To make the cheese sauce, place a medium cast-iron pan on the EGG cooking grid and add the butter. Melt the butter and whisk in the flour for 2 to 3 minutes, until it is completely incorporated and makes a light roux. Add the heavy cream and bring to a boil, continuing to whisk for 3 to 4 minutes, until slightly thickened. Add the seasonings and cheese and whisk and cook until thickened to your desired sauce consistency.

Serve the pork belly immediately over the top of yellow corn tortilla chips, followed with the cheese sauce, and finish by drizzling with the reserved barbecue sauce.

Smoked Chicken Chili

Makes 8 to 10 servings

A nice piping-hot and comforting bowl of chili is great for when it's cold outside or you just want to eat something that warms your heart, stomach, and soul. The smoked chicken thighs, Mexican chili powder, and charred poblano give this particular chili a nice smoky and satisfying flavor that can be achieved only on the EGG. The sweet corn gives it a surprisingly sweet pop and crunch that really sets off this chili party. Enjoy with my Bacon–Cheddar Corn Bread (page 45) to help sop up all that goodness!

3 pounds skinless chicken thighs

1 cup apple wood chips, soaked for 1 hour in 2 cups water

BRINE

4 cups water

¼ cup salt

½ cup granulated sugar

CHILI

3 tablespoons olive oil

1 large yellow onion, small diced

2 green onions, green and white parts minced

3 cloves garlic, minced

1 medium red bell pepper, seeded and small diced

2 ears sweet yellow corn, shucked, kernels cut

1 poblano pepper, charred and peeled, small diced

1 teaspoon kosher salt

1 teaspoon black pepper

2 teaspoons ground cumin

2 tablespoons Mexican chili powder

1 teaspoon smoked paprika

1 teaspoon granulated garlic

1 teaspoon granulated onion

3 tablespoons tomato paste

1 (12-ounce) can IPA beer

40 ounces chicken broth

2 tablespoons Worcestershire sauce

2 (15.5-ounce) cans cannellini beans

TOPPINGS

½ cup minced white onion

½ cup minced green onions, only green parts

1 cup shredded cheddar cheese

10 ounces sour cream

(continued)

(continued from page 35)

Rinse and pat dry the chicken thighs, then place them in a large resealable plastic bag or plastic container. To make the brine, place all of the ingredients in a large pan on the stovetop and whisk well until incorporated. Bring to a boil over high heat, then remove from the heat and cool to room temperature. Pour the cooled brine over the thighs and seal the bag or container tightly, removing any air. Brine overnight in the fridge, or for at least 4 hours.

Prepare the EGG to cook indirect with a drip pan at 375°F. Drain the wood chips and place them in the EGG over the hot coals. Remove the chicken thighs from the brine, rinse, and pat dry. Grill the chicken thighs on the EGG cooking grid for about 15 minutes per side, or until cooked through and golden brown. Remove them from the EGG. Once cool enough to handle, thinly slice or shred the chicken and set aside.

To make the chili, place a large cast-iron Dutch oven on the EGG cooking grid and add the olive oil. Sauté the yellow and green onions along with the garlic and pepper for 1 to 2 minutes, until fragrant. Then add the corn kernels and poblano pepper and sauté for an additional 3 minutes. Add all of the dry seasonings and sauté for 2 minutes, until fragrant. Add the tomato paste and continue sautéing for an additional 2 minutes. Add the beer and cook until reduced by half in volume, 4 to 5 minutes. Stir in the chicken broth and bring to a boil. Add the chicken, Worcestershire sauce, and a pinch of salt and pepper. Cover with a lid and continue to cook for 10 minutes. Add the beans and continue to cook for another 20 minutes. Season to taste with salt and pepper. Top each serving as desired with the white onion, green onions, cheese, and sour cream. Serve with a hearty slice of the Bacon–Cheddar Corn Bread.

CHAPTER

3

SIDE ACTS

(SIDES)

If the main course is Gladys Knight, then the sides are the Pips! They support, harmonize, add balance, and complement and contrast the flavors of the main course. And sometimes the sides are so good they can even venture off and become solo acts themselves. All of the sides in this chapter are designed to be paired with many of the main courses. So feel free to experiment and mix and match your favorite sides with your favorite entrées or just cook a bunch of sides up and enjoy that too. After all, eating great food is always a constructive way to spend your time. Either way . . . get ready for these sides to shine like the Pips that they are!

Lobster Mac 'n' Cheese

Makes 8 to 10 servings

I'd like to think of myself as a mac 'n' cheese connoisseur of sorts . . . The different combinations of cheese and pasta are LITERALLY endless. But this one truly puts a twinkle in my eye and a smile in my stomach with the blend of sharp cheddar and nutty Parmesan and the gradual build of mild heat from the pepper jack. These are the soul mate to the garlic butter–bathed sweet and briny lobster meat folded into the pasta. I find that the cheese sauce adheres better to the spiral shape of the cavatappi pasta. And I don't know about you, but the more cheese that clings to my fork, the better the world is. I truly feel that with each bite of the crusty Parmesan bruléed on top, an angel gets their wings. Yep . . . it's that good!

4 ounces unsalted butter

4 cloves garlic, minced

3 pounds raw lobster, claws and knuckle meat

¼ cup coarsely chopped fresh Italian parsley

2 teaspoons kosher salt

1 teaspoon white pepper

4 tablespoons all-purpose flour

3 cups heavy cream

2 cups freshly grated Parmesan cheese, divided

2 cups shredded sharp cheddar cheese, divided

1 cup shredded pepper jack cheese

½ teaspoon black pepper

½ teaspoon smoked paprika

½ teaspoon granulated garlic

½ teaspoon granulated onion

¼ teaspoon cayenne pepper

1 pound cavatappi pasta, cooked al dente

Prepare the EGG to cook direct at 450°F. Place a 12-inch cast-iron pan on the EGG cooking grid and add the butter and garlic. Once the butter is melted, add the lobster, parsley, salt, and pepper and stir. Poach the lobster lightly for 5 to 6 minutes, until bright red. Season to taste if needed with additional salt and pepper. Remove the lobster to a separate plate and set aside, reserving the liquid.

Bring the reserved liquid to a rapid boil and whisk in the flour until it creates a blond roux. Add the heavy cream while continuously whisking. Bring to a boil and stir until slightly thickened. Whisk in 1 cup of the Parmesan, 1 cup of the sharp cheddar, the pepper jack, and all of the seasonings until melted and smooth.

Remove the pan from the EGG and place the convEGGtor in the EGG. Add the pasta, lobster meat, and remaining 1 cup sharp cheddar and use a rubber spatula to mix thoroughly. Top with the remaining 1 cup Parmesan. Place the pan back into the EGG and continue to cook for an additional 20 minutes until the mac 'n' cheese is bubbly and nicely browned.

Grilled Carrots with Balsamic-Honey Glaze, Feta, and Sunflower Seeds

Makes 6 servings

The beautiful thing about the EGG is that it does magic and creates wonderment by grilling vegetables as well. Sweet rainbow carrots get charred and brushed with balsamic-honey glaze and finished with crumbly feta cheese and roasted sunflower seeds. I'm a BIG fan of contrasting flavors, textures, and temperatures . . . It just makes food that more exciting. Sweet, salty, acid, soft, creamy, crunchy . . . these carrots really got it going on!

GLAZE

1 cup balsamic vinegar

1 cup honey

2 tablespoons minced shallots

CARROTS

2 pounds organic rainbow carrots, tops trimmed and blanched for 5 minutes in salted water

2 cloves garlic, minced

Pinch of kosher salt and black pepper

2 tablespoons olive oil

4 ounces crumbled feta cheese

3 tablespoons salted, roasted sunflower seeds

¼ cup chopped fresh cilantro

Prepare the EGG to cook direct at 400°F. To make the glaze, on the stovetop, place the vinegar, honey, and shallots in a small saucepot. Bring to a boil, then reduce to a simmer and continue to cook for 12 to 14 minutes, until reduced to a glaze consistency. Set aside and cool to room temperature.

To make the carrots, toss them with the garlic, salt and pepper, and olive oil in a large bowl. Place them on the EGG cooking grid and cook on one side for 4 to 5 minutes, until slightly blistered. Flip the carrots over and brush with the glaze. Continue to cook for about another 3 minutes. Flip them again so you can glaze the other side. Continue to cook for another minute, until lacquered.

Remove the carrots from the EGG and drizzle them with the remaining glaze and top them with the cheese, sunflower seeds, and cilantro.

Mexican Street Corn Skewer

Makes 8 servings

You don't have to look very far in Mexico to find this traditional creamy, savory, and spicy street fair staple. Elote translates to "corn on the cob." It's slathered with lime mayo and topped with cotija cheese, and the citrus notes of the lime mayo amplify the sweetness of the corn. Doing a quick brine on the corn, rubbing it with olive oil, and grilling it on the EGG all create a depth in flavor of sweetness and saltiness. One thing about Mexican street corn is that it tends to be a little messy, so my recipe includes skewering the corn after grilling. This will help keep all the toppings from falling all over the place and instead encourage them to go in your mouth . . . where they belong!

8 ears sweet yellow corn, shucked and cleaned and cut in half horizontally

BRINE
1 gallon warm water
¼ cup kosher salt
½ cup granulated sugar

MAYONNAISE
1 cup mayonnaise
Juice of ½ lime
½ teaspoon smoked paprika
½ teaspoon granulated garlic
Kosher salt and black pepper

TOPPINGS
½ cup olive oil
1 cup crumbled cotija cheese
Smoked paprika, for garnish
½ cup chopped fresh cilantro, for garnish
16 skewers

For the brine, place all of the ingredients in a large, deep pan, whisk until dissolved, and add the corn so that it's completely covered. Brine for 30 to 45 minutes.

Meanwhile, to make the mayonnaise, combine all of the ingredients in a small bowl and whisk together. Season with salt and pepper to taste. Set aside.

Prepare the EGG to cook direct at 425°F. Remove the corn from the brine, shake off excess water, and coat each ear with olive oil using a brush. Place the ears on the EGG cooking grid. Grill on all sides for 6 to 8 minutes, until lightly charred and golden. Remove the corn from the EGG and insert a skewer in one end of each ear. To assemble, brush each ear with lime mayo, add some cheese on all sides, dust with paprika, and garnish with cilantro.

Bacon–Cheddar Corn Bread with Salted Honey Butter

Makes 8 servings

Living in Atlanta, Georgia, for the last eighteen years, it's fair to say that I've had my share of corn bread . . . many times. There's always the debate over savory or sweet corn bread, but I say why not both? My corn bread is chock-full of sweet corn kernels that explode in your mouth, cheddar cheese that gives it an alluring cheesy pull, and salty, savory bacon. It's done up in a cast-iron pan on the EGG for a nice crispy crust and served with salted honey butter (page 38). What's not to love? Finally, a corn bread that EVERYONE can enjoy! You can thank me later . . . or now . . . Now works good too.

CORN BREAD

3 tablespoons vegetable oil, divided

5 strips bacon, diced

1 cup shucked fresh corn kernels

Pinch of kosher salt

2 cups White Lily Enriched Self-Rising White Cornmeal Mix

½ cup granulated sugar

1½ cups buttermilk

1 large egg, beaten

½ cup freshly shredded sharp cheddar cheese

HONEY BUTTER

8 ounces unsalted butter, at room temperature

5 tablespoons honey

1 teaspoon kosher salt

Prepare the EGG to cook indirect with a drip pan at 425°F. To make the corn bread, place a 9-inch cast-iron pan on the EGG cooking grid and add 1 tablespoon of the vegetable oil. Add the bacon and cook for 5 to 7 minutes, until crispy and browned. Remove the bacon with a slotted spoon to drain on a paper towel–lined plate. Reserve the bacon fat in the pan. Add the corn and the salt and sauté for 2 minutes, until lightly browned. Remove the pan from the EGG, and remove the corn from the pan with a slotted spoon, set aside. Don't wipe out the pan.

In a large bowl whisk together the cornmeal mix and sugar. Then add the buttermilk and egg and whisk again. Last, add the bacon, corn, and cheese and stir until well incorporated. Place the pan back on the EGG for 3 to 5 minutes to get hot. Add the remaining 2 tablespoons vegetable oil and swirl around to coat the entire pan. Pour the batter into the hot pan and close the lid of the EGG. Bake for 25 to 30 minutes, until a toothpick comes out clean and the top of the corn bread is golden brown.

While the bread is baking, make the honey butter. Place all of the ingredients in a medium bowl and use an electric mixer to incorporate thoroughly. Serve the bread warm with lots of honey butter.

Sesame Asparagus with Soy Vinaigrette

Makes 4 servings

The big, bold flavors of Asian cuisine are something I grew up enjoying in the tristate area and absolutely loved. Whenever I can, I like to sneak 'em in the Big Green Egg mix! Asparagus is the perfect vessel for this grilled vegetable side because it takes on the flavors of what it's prepared with so very well. And when it's tossed with garlic and olive oil, charred on the EGG, and glazed with a soy vinaigrette, the subtle nuances of soy, sesame, honey, and the pungent-peppery mustard deliver a well-balanced bite as the sesame seeds explode in your mouth with each bite.

VINAIGRETTE

¼ cup soy sauce

3 tablespoons rice wine vinegar

2 tablespoons yellow mustard

3 tablespoons honey

¼ teaspoon sesame oil

Pinch of crushed red pepper

Kosher salt and black pepper

ASPARAGUS

1 pound jumbo asparagus, trimmed, and blanched in salted water for 2 minutes

2 tablespoons olive oil

2 cloves garlic, minced

1 teaspoon kosher salt

½ teaspoon black pepper

2 tablespoons chopped fresh cilantro, for garnish

1 teaspoon sesame seeds, for garnish

Prepare the EGG to cook direct at 450°F. To make the vinaigrette, place all of the ingredients in a medium bowl and whisk until well incorporated. Season to taste with salt and pepper. Set aside.

To make the asparagus, toss it in a large bowl with the olive oil, garlic, and salt and pepper and then grill it on the EGG cooking grid for 2 to 3 minutes per side. As the asparagus cooks, glaze it with the vinaigrette, twice on both sides, until slightly charred. Remove from the EGG. Drizzle with more vinaigrette, garnish with cilantro and sesame seeds, and serve.

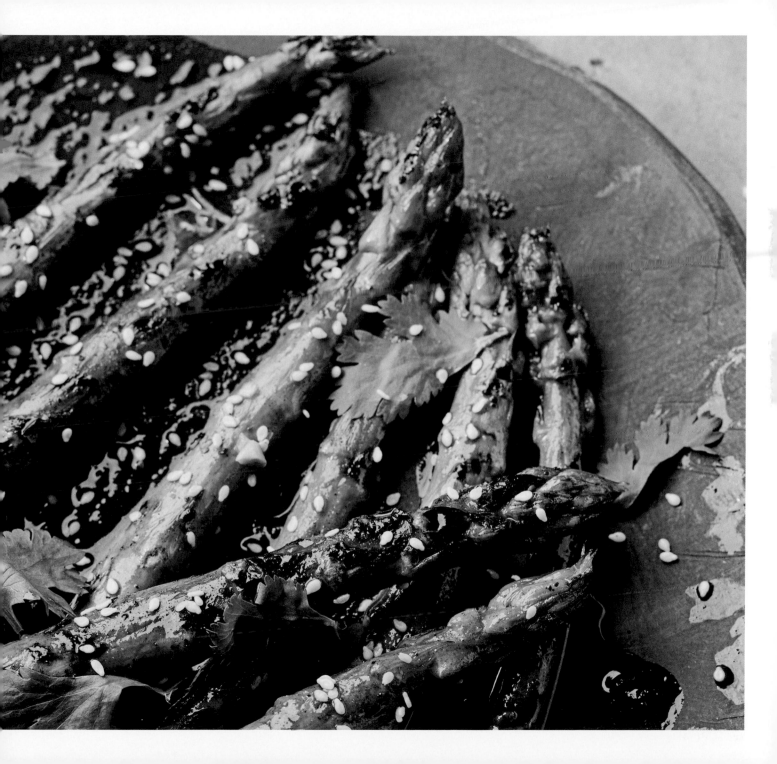

Wok-Fried Vegetable Lo Mein

Makes 8 to 10 servings

Chinese takeout was always a special treat growing up as a kid in New Jersey, especially since my mom always made amazing home-cooked meals 99.9 percent of the time. On the rare occasion when we'd indulge, lo mein was always one of my go-tos. Perfectly cooked noodles with crisp, flavorful vegetables, dripping with sticky umami-bomb stir-fry sauce, remind me of those special evenings with my mom. And what better way to re-create those amazing flavors than on the EGG with a wok? So jump right into this "takeout fakeout"!

SAUCE

1½ cups vegetable broth

¼ cup packed light brown sugar

½ cup mirin
  (sweet Japanese cooking wine)

⅛ cup sweet chili sauce

1 tablespoon sriracha

¼ teaspoon sesame oil

2 tablespoons cornstarch

LO MEIN

3 tablespoons vegetable oil

½ medium yellow onion, small diced

1 medium red bell pepper, seeded
  and julienned

3 cloves garlic, thinly sliced

1 teaspoon peeled and freshly grated
  ginger root

4 ounces thinly sliced shiitake
  mushrooms

¼ pound snow peas, blanched in salted
  water for 1 minute

Kosher salt and black pepper

28 ounces lo mein noodles, cooked
  al dente

¼ cup chopped fresh cilantro,
  for garnish

Prepare the EGG to cook direct with a wok setup at 425°F. To make the sauce, place all of the ingredients in a medium bowl and whisk until well incorporated. Set aside.

To make the lo mein, add the vegetable oil to the wok and sauté the onion, pepper, garlic, and ginger for about 1 minute. Then add the mushrooms, snow peas, and a pinch of salt and pepper, and continue sautéing for 3 to 4 minutes. Add the sauce and bring to a boil. Continue to cook until the mixture thickens to your desired consistency. Add the cooked noodles and stir fry for 3 to 5 minutes, until hot and fully coated with the sauce. Top with the cilantro and serve.

Wok-Fried Beef Fried Rice

Makes 4 servings

And the beat goes on . . . Or, in this case, the BEEF goes on . . . as in beef fried rice. The occasional Chinese takeout dinners I enjoyed in my childhood would never be complete without an order of beef fried rice. Just thinking about a bowl of nutty fried rice, bursting at the seams with flavors of soy, sesame, fresh green onions, lightly fried egg, sweet stir-fried yellow onions, and perfectly cooked strips of beef, makes me drool. Here I've spiced things up a little with the inclusion of tomato paste and sriracha to add more in-depth flavor. It's the perfect side to, well, anything!

2 tablespoons plus 2 teaspoons canola oil, divided

3 large eggs, beaten

1 pound ground beef

1 teaspoon salt

1 teaspoon black pepper

1 teaspoon sesame oil

½ teaspoon chili oil, optional

½ cup finely minced yellow onion

2 tablespoons chopped green onions, white and green parts

2 cloves garlic, minced

1 cup frozen vegetable medley (carrots, corn, green beans), thawed

1 tablespoon tomato paste

1 tablespoon sriracha

2 cups cooked white rice, cold

2 teaspoons soy sauce

¼ cup chopped fresh cilantro

Prepare the EGG to cook direct with a wok setup at 425°F. Place 1 teaspoon of the canola oil in the wok and add the eggs. Cook the eggs for about 30 seconds, or until fluffy and lightly cooked. Be careful not to overcook them. Remove the eggs from the wok, set aside, and carefully wipe the wok clean with a paper towel. Add 2 tablespoons of canola oil and the ground beef to the wok. Add the salt and pepper and sauté for 5 to 7 minutes, until brown and fully cooked through.

Remove the ground beef from the wok and set aside. Add the sesame oil, chili oil (if using), and the remaining 1 teaspoon canola oil to the wok. Sauté the yellow and green onions and garlic until caramelized. Add the vegetables and a pinch of salt and pepper. Continue to cook for 3 to 4 minutes, until hot and lightly caramelized. Add the ground beef back into the wok, along with the tomato paste and sriracha. Sauté for 2 to 3 minutes, until the tomato paste and sriracha become fragrant.

Add the rice and soy sauce and stir fry until the rice is thoroughly heated and starts to slightly brown. Add the eggs and cilantro and stir fry until well incorporated with the other ingredients. Serve straight from the wok. If needed, season to taste with additional salt and pepper.

CHAPTER 4

MAIN ATTRACTIONS

(ENTRÉES)

It's time for the Big Show: Entrées . . . the MAIN ATTRACTION! Let's be honest . . . As much as your neighbors, family, and friends want to come over and see your newly renovated basement or the doghouse you just built for your family puppy, Peaches, what they really came for is . . . GRILLED MEAT! Flavorful rubs, tongue-teasing sauces, drool-worthy marinades, steaks, chops, wings, roasts . . . You name it, I got it. And now you have it too. Let's light that EGG up and get ready to create some magic. Your guests are starting to get hungry . . .

Chili–Grilled Lamb Chops with Mango Chutney

Makes 4 servings

You don't have to look too far in Jamaica for the Indian influence in the local fare. After all, the beautiful island is part of the group of island countries dubbed the West Indies because of their cultural makeup and the indigenous people hailing from the Indies (India), the East Indies of South Asia, and Southeast Asia. These succulent lamb chops are marinated with chiu chow chili oil, lending a salty-spicy note that screams Asian cuisine. Tropical mangos are plentiful in Jamaica, and the people of Jamaica are no stranger to curry. The sweet and sour notes found in the mango chutney are complemented by the inclusion of the warm curry spices and pop of sweetness from the golden raisins. I grilled up these beauties at EGGtoberfest in 2019, and we had a long line that remained until we handed out the last bite. These are the perfect finger food to switch things up with a Caribbean flair at your next summer barbecue.

CHUTNEY

2 tablespoons canola oil

½ cup small-diced yellow onion

½ cup small-diced red bell pepper

½ teaspoon peeled and freshly grated
    ginger root

1½ teaspoons curry powder

1½ cups medium-diced fresh mango,
    or frozen mango, thawed

½ cup golden raisins

1¼ cups apple cider vinegar

1 cup packed light brown sugar

LAMB CHOPS

½ cup olive oil

2 tablespoons minced garlic

2 tablespoons chiu chow–style chili oil

2 tablespoons chopped fresh Italian
    flat leaf parsley

1½ tablespoons Goya Adobo seasoning

2 teaspoons paprika

2 teaspoons black pepper

1 teaspoon granulated garlic

1 teaspoon granulated onion

12 (1-inch-thick) French-cut lamb rib chops

Vegetable oil, for the cooking grid

Prepare the EGG to cook direct at 400°F. To make the chutney, place a medium cast-iron pan on the EGG cooking grid and add the canola oil. Add the onion, pepper, ginger, and curry powder to the pan. Sauté for 5 to 6 minutes, until the vegetables are tender and caramelized and the curry has cooked. Add the mango and raisins to the pan and sauté for an additional 3 to 4 minutes. Add the vinegar and brown sugar, stirring together until the ingredients come to a boil.

Once the mixture has come to a boil, move the saucepot to a cooler spot on the EGG. Continue to cook for 10 to 12 minutes more, until the chutney is reduced to a syrupy consistency. Remove the pot from the EGG. Set aside.

To make the lamb chops, add the olive oil, garlic, chili oil, and parsley to a medium bowl. Whisk until well

incorporated. In a small bowl, whisk the dry ingredients together and season both sides of the lamb chops with the dry spices, and then toss thoroughly in the chili–olive oil mixture. Wrap the bowl with plastic wrap and marinate the lamb chops overnight in the fridge, or for at least 3 hours.

Prepare the EGG to cook direct at 400°F. Remove the lamb chops from the fridge and allow them to come to room temperature for about 30 minutes. Oil the EGG cooking grid with vegetable oil to prevent sticking. Grill the chops on both sides for 4 to 6 minutes for medium doneness, until slightly charred. Serve immediately with the chutney.

Pork Carnitas with Arepas and Salsa Verde

Makes 10 to 12 servings

Carnitas, carnitas, carnitas . . . why are you soooo yummy? Let me count the ways! The word "carnitas" literally means "little meats" in Spanish, but this dish is BIG on flavors. This is the Mexican version of pulled pork is slathered in oregano, cumin, orange, onion, and fresh garlic and then slow roasted in a Dutch oven until it's so tender it melts in your mouth (move over M&Ms . . .). Crisped up in a cast-iron pan with its natural juices, for the perfect 1-2 knockout combination of crispy, crusty, soft, and salty goodness, piled high on a deep-fried arepa! Put on your stretchy-waistband eating pants, because you're gonna need 'em when you make these.

RUB

1 tablespoon dried oregano

1 tablespoon ground cumin

1 teaspoon smoked paprika

¼ teaspoon granulated onion

2 tablespoons olive oil

PORK

1 (5-pound) bone-in pork butt

2 tablespoons kosher salt

1 tablespoon black pepper

1 large yellow onion, peeled and sliced

5 cloves garlic, minced

1 large jalapeño, seeded and sliced

2 green onions, green and white parts minced

Juice from 2 navel oranges

SALSA VERDE

1 pound tomatillos, husked, washed, dried, and quartered

3 cloves garlic

1 jalapeño, including seeds, halved

¼ cup small-diced yellow onion

2 tablespoons olive oil

1 teaspoon kosher salt

½ teaspoon black pepper

¼ cup chopped fresh cilantro

Juice of ½ lime

1 teaspoon red wine vinegar

Kosher salt and black pepper

AREPAS

2 cups instant yellow corn masa flour

1½ cups water

¼ teaspoon kosher salt, plus more for sprinkling

3 cups vegetable oil

2 ounces crumbled cotija cheese, for serving

Prepare the EGG to cook indirect at 350°F. Make the rub by whisking all of the ingredients together in a small bowl. Rinse and pat dry the pork butt and then season it with the salt and pepper. Sprinkle the rub on all sides of the pork and then place it in a Dutch oven. Cover it with the yellow onion, garlic, jalapeño, green onions, and orange juice. Cover the Dutch oven with the lid and place on the EGG cooking grid. Cook for 4 to 5 hours, until the meat is fork tender and falling apart.

The salsa verde can be made ahead of time and refrigerated until ready to use. To make the salsa verde, place all of the ingredients, except the cilantro, lime juice, and vinegar, into a medium bowl and toss the ingredients thoroughly, with a pinch of salt and pepper. Place the mixture in a 12-inch cast-iron pan, or on a half sheet pan, on the EGG cooking grid to cook indirect at 375°F. Roast the vegetables for 20 to 25 minutes, until browned and caramelized. Remove the pan from the EGG and place the vegetables in a food processor, using the chopping/mixing blade. Add the cilantro, lime juice, and vinegar; blend until the mixture forms a loose salsa-like consistency. Season to taste with salt and pepper, and set aside.

Remove the carnitas from the Dutch oven and pull apart in big chunks. DON'T shred it too much and DON'T discard the braising juices.

Prepare the EGG to cook direct at 400°F. Place a large 12-inch cast-iron pan on the EGG cooking grid and panfry the carnitas in the braising juices until golden brown and the fat has crisped up. Flip the pieces when the meat starts to form a crust. Remove the pan from the EGG and set aside.

To make the arepas, combine the masa flour, water, and salt in a medium-sized bowl. Work into a smooth masa dough. Take golf ball–sized pieces of dough and roll them into small, smooth balls. Using a tortilla press with parchment paper or wax paper on both sides, press to ¼-inch thickness, and about 3 to 4 inches diameter. Alternately, you can use a dinner plate with parchment paper on both sides of the masa dough to achieve the same result. Repeat with the remaining balls.

Place a wok on the EGG cooking grid and carefully add the vegetable oil. Use a thermometer to make sure the oil temperature is between 350°F and 375°F. Deep-fry the arepas in batches of 3 until golden brown, flipping them after 60 to 90 seconds and then cooking them for another 60 to 90 seconds. Remove the arepas and place them on a paper towel–lined plate to drain. Immediately sprinkle salt on the arepas while they are hot. Repeat with the remaining arepas.

To assemble, place a heaping spoonful of carnitas with juice on top of an arepa, drizzle with salsa verde, and finish with a little crumble of cheese.

Grilled Double-Cut Pork Chops with Maple-Pecan Butter

Makes 2 servings

Pork truly is nature's "meat candy"! The natural sweetness found in pork is so provocative and seductive, and a quality double-cut pork chop is a prime example. The sweetness and tenderness are amplified by the brine of fresh herbs and aromatics. Then these are chargrilled on the EGG and finished with a sweet and nutty maple-pecan butter. Mmmmm . . . I'll have two, please!

2 bone-in double-cut, thick-cut pork chops (about 1½ inches thick)

BRINE

3 cups water

½ cup granulated sugar

2 tablespoons kosher salt

2 cloves garlic, peeled and smashed

2 sprigs fresh rosemary

2 sprigs fresh thyme

1 teaspoon green peppercorns

BUTTER

12 tablespoons unsalted butter, at room temperature

4 tablespoons pure maple syrup

1 teaspoon minced fresh chives

¼ cup finely chopped salted and roasted pecans

Kosher salt and black pepper

Place the pork chops in a large resealable plastic bag. To make the brine, place a medium-sized saucepot on the stovetop. Add all of the ingredients and bring to a boil. Remove the pot from the stovetop and cool the brine to room temperature. Once the brine has cooled, pour it over the chops. Close the bag tightly and let the pork chops brine overnight in the refrigerator.

Remove the pork chops from the brine and pat them dry on both sides with a paper towel. Allow them to come to room temperature for 20 to 30 minutes.

Meanwhile, to make the butter, combine all of the ingredients in a medium bowl. Using an electric mixer, whip the ingredients together and season to taste with salt and pepper. Set aside.

Prepare the EGG to cook direct at 425°F. On the EGG cooking grid, grill the pork chops on one side for 5 to 6 minutes, until a nicely seared and brown crust forms. Flip and cook on the other side, for another 5 to 6 minutes, until an internal temperature of 140°F is reached for medium doneness. Cook for a few minutes longer for well done. Remove the pork chops from the EGG and allow them to rest on a wire rack–lined sheet pan for 7 to 8 minutes. The resting allows the juices to redistribute and continue carryover cooking to a perfect 145°F medium doneness. Serve with the butter.

Guinness Barbecue Lamb Breast

Makes 4 servings

Baby back ribs, spareribs, beef ribs, short ribs . . . all are magically delicious. But have you ever had LAMB RIBS? (I'll wait while you pick your jaw up from the ground . . .). Yes, lamb ribs. They come from the lamb breast, which is essentially lamb belly, with the rib still attached to it. For texture, I would describe it as a cross between pork belly and a sparerib, but fattier and deeper in flavor. Slow roasted on the EGG until fork tender, with warm spices like cumin, cinnamon, and paprika, the lamb takes really well to big flavors; then it's glazed with the sweet, smoky, and bittersweet notes of the Guinness barbecue sauce. Forget the napkins . . . this one is finger-licking good!

RUB

2 tablespoons kosher salt

1 tablespoon black pepper

1½ tablespoons granulated sugar

1 teaspoon smoked paprika

1 teaspoon ground cinnamon

½ teaspoon granulated garlic

½ teaspoon granulated onion

1 teaspoon ground cumin

2½ pounds bone-in lamb breast

½ cup apple juice

SAUCE

1 (11.2-ounce) bottle Guinness stout

1 cup ketchup

⅓ cup packed light brown sugar

2 tablespoons apple cider vinegar

½ teaspoon smoked paprika

½ teaspoon granulated garlic

Prepare the EGG to cook indirect with a drip pan at 325°F. To make the rub, place all of the ingredients in a small bowl and whisk together until well incorporated. Season the lamb breast with the rub and allow it to come to room temperature for 30 to 45 minutes.

Place the lamb on the EGG cooking grid, fat side up, and cook for 1 hour. Flip the fat side down and cook for another 30 minutes. Remove the lamb from the EGG, and double-wrap with butcher paper, pour apple juice over lamb, then return it to the EGG to cook with the fat side up for an additional 30 minutes.

The sauce can be made in advance up to 5 days, and kept refrigerated. To make the sauce, prepare the EGG to cook direct at 400°F. Place a medium cast-iron saucepot on the EGG cooking grid and add the beer. Bring to a boil and reduce by half in volume, 4 to 5 minutes. Add the rest of the ingredients and continue to cook for 3 to 4 minutes more. Cool to room temperature.

Remove the lamb from the butcher paper and place it back on the EGG. Glaze it with the sauce on both sides, until lacquered and sticky. Remove it from the EGG and serve.

Sriracha–Honey Barbecue Baby Back Ribs

Makes 6 servings

Sriracha hot sauce has gained immense popularity in the last two decades. It adds great flavor and complements a lot of different foods. So why not put it on baby back ribs? These ribs have a sticky and sweet barbecue sauce with sriracha, honey, ketchup, molasses, and rice wine vinegar (page 50). Asia meets Southern barbecue with this recipe. And it's pretty darn tasty!

RIBS

2 racks baby back ribs (about 3 pounds)

2 cups apple juice, divided

2 tablespoons honey, divided

1 cup cherry wood chips, soaked for
    1 hour in 2 cups water

RUB

2 tablespoons kosher salt

2 tablespoons light brown sugar

1 tablespoon smoked paprika

1 tablespoon black pepper

1 teaspoon granulated garlic

1 teaspoon granulated onion

1 teaspoon za'atar

2 teaspoons Chinese five spice

SAUCE

1 cup ketchup

¼ cup sriracha

½ cup honey

¼ cup rice wine vinegar

1 tablespoon molasses

¼ teaspoon granulated garlic

Prepare the EGG to cook indirect with a drip pan at 300°F. Remove the membrane from the back of the ribs and pat the ribs dry with a paper towel. To make the rub, place all of the ingredients in a small bowl and mix well. Season the ribs liberally on both sides with the rub and allow them to come to room temperature for 30 minutes.

Drain the wood chips and place them in the EGG over the hot coals. Place the ribs in the center of the EGG cooking grid, fatty side up, and cook for 2 hours.

Meanwhile, to make the sauce, place a medium-sized saucepot on the stovetop. Add all of the ingredients and bring to a boil. Continue to cook for 4 to 5 minutes, until all of the ingredients come together and form a sauce-like consistency. Remove the pot from the stovetop and cool the sauce to room temperature.

After the ribs have cooked for 2 hours, flip the fat side down and cook for 1 hour. Then double-wrap each rack of ribs in butcher paper and pour 1 cup of the apple juice and 1 tablespoon of the honey over each rack separately. Return the ribs to the EGG and cook for an additional hour.

Remove the ribs from the butcher paper and place back on the EGG, glazing each rack with sauce on each side. Allow 3 to 4 minutes for each side and coat each side twice for the ribs to get sticky and lacquered. Remove the ribs from the EGG and serve.

Jamaican Jerk Chicken with Pineapple-Habanero Sauce

Makes 8 to 10 servings

You know you've arrived in Jamaica when you see the street vendors and their hollowed-out makeshift barrel smokers. Smoking . . . you've guessed it: Jamaican jerk chicken, the national dish of Jamaica. The chicken is marinated in Scotch bonnet pepper, green onions, garlic, ginger, thyme, soy sauce, and allspice and packed full of flavor. Then it's slowwwwww smoked/grilled over pimento wood, the authentic way. Apple wood is a good substitution if pimento wood isn't available. This recipe follows the same tradition and delivers those same flavors of the islands, hot off the EGG. Moderate tongue-tingling spice and warm and inviting flavors of the chicken are complemented with the sweet and jammy tropical flavors of the pineapple-habanero sauce. Grab your flip-flops and sunglasses and get ready to have your taste buds transported to the beaches of Jamaica.

SAUCE

1 tablespoon olive oil

1 habanero pepper, seeded and minced

2 ounces spiced rum

6 ounces bottled pineapple juice

1½ cups small-diced pineapple

⅓ cup granulated sugar

MARINADE

½ cup soy sauce

3 medium green onions, coarsely chopped

2 Scotch bonnet chiles or habaneros, with seeds, halved

3 cloves garlic

1 tablespoon peeled and freshly grated ginger root

1 tablespoon ground allspice

1 teaspoon brown sugar

1 tablespoon coarsely ground pepper

½ teaspoon ground cloves

¼ teaspoon ground nutmeg

1 teaspoon ground thyme

1 teaspoon kosher salt

1 tablespoon vegetable oil

4 pounds chicken thighs or leg quarters, cleaned and trimmed

1 cup pimento or apple wood chips, soaked for 1 hour in 2 cups water

To make the sauce on the stovetop, on medium-high heat, add the olive oil and habanero to a medium-sized saucepot and lightly sauté for 2 to 3 minutes, until tender. Add the rum to the pot and reduce the volume by one-third. Then add the pineapple juice and bring to a boil. Add the pineapple and sugar and cook for 5 to 7 minutes, until the pineapple becomes glazed and syrupy. Remove from the stovetop.

For the marinade, combine all of the ingredients in a large bowl until fully incorporated. Place the chicken in the bowl and gently toss, making sure it is fully coated. Cover the bowl with plastic wrap or place the marinated chicken in a resealable plastic bag. Place the chicken in the fridge and marinate overnight, or for at least 6 hours.

Prepare the EGG to cook indirect with a drip pan at 375°F. Drain the wood chips and place them in the EGG over the hot coals. Remove the chicken from the marinade and discard the rest. Place the chicken skin side up on the EGG cooking grid and cook for 15 to 20 minutes. Then flip the chicken skin side down and continue to cook for another 15 to 20 minutes. Flip it to the skin side up again and cook until golden brown and the internal temperature reads 165°F. Remove the chicken from the EGG and serve.

Lemon–Herb Spatchcock Chicken

Makes 4 servings

Lemony, herbaceous, juicy, delicious spatchcock chicken generously rubbed with rosemary, thyme, parsley, garlic, and lemon zest . . . your mouth will LITERALLY be filled with excitement once you take a bite. By removing the spine of the chicken and grilling it whole, you allow the white and dark meat to cook evenly and you end up with super crispy chicken skin! You're right. . . . I should've just led with the "super crispy chicken skin" . . . I know. The citrus notes of the chicken complement the fresh herbs, and then it's all perfectly grilled on the EGG.

1 (4-pound) fryer chicken

Kosher salt and black pepper

OIL

8 sprigs fresh thyme, leaves removed and minced

4 sprigs fresh rosemary, leaves removed and minced

6 cloves garlic, minced

¼ cup minced fresh Italian parsley

Juice of ½ lemon

1 teaspoon finely grated lemon zest

½ teaspoon crushed red pepper

1 teaspoon kosher salt

1 teaspoon black pepper

Rinse and pat dry the chicken. Using kitchen shears or a knife, remove the backbone of the chicken, lay the breast side up, and then flatten the chicken with your hands. Liberally season both sides with salt and pepper. Allow the chicken to dry brine by leaving it uncovered in the fridge overnight. This process adds flavors, releases moisture, and creates super crispy chicken skin when roasted.

To make the oil, combine all of the ingredients in a medium bowl and whisk until fully incorporated. Set aside.

When ready to cook, remove the chicken from the fridge and slather with the oil on both sides. Allow it to come to room temperature for about 30 to 40 minutes.

Prepare the EGG to cook indirect with a drip pan at 375°F. Cook the chicken breast side up on the EGG cooking grid for 30 minutes, then flip over to continue cooking for 30 minutes, until the internal temperature in the breast reaches 160°F and the chicken skin is crispy. Remove the chicken from the EGG and allow it to rest for 12 to 15 minutes before carving. Carryover cooking will bring the internal temperature to 165°F and allow the juices to distribute evenly.

Honey–Thyme Grilled Quail

Makes 4 servings

As a graduate of Le Cordon Bleu College of Culinary Arts, I have learned a lot of traditional French recipes and techniques. The small, plump, and super flavorful quail can be readily found in classic French cuisine. By spatchcocking these tasty little birds, seasoning them with herbes de Provence (a mixture of dried herbs, typical of the cuisine found in the Provence region of France), and basting them with a honey-thyme glaze, it's truly the perfect marriage of savory and sweet. And your name will go down forever in the history books as the person who made superb grilled quail at a summer barbecue. Don't you want to be that person?!

4 (¼-pound) whole quails
    (total weight about 1 pound)

RUB
1 tablespoon kosher salt
1 teaspoon black pepper
¼ teaspoon smoked paprika
¼ teaspoon granulated garlic
¼ teaspoon herbes de Provence

GLAZE
2 tablespoons olive oil
2 cloves garlic, minced
2 tablespoons minced shallots
4 sprigs fresh thyme, leaves
    removed and minced
¼ cup honey
1 cup chicken broth

Prepare the EGG to cook direct at 375°F. Use kitchen shears or a knife to remove the spine from the quails and then flatten the quails, breast side up, with your hands. To make the rub, add all of the ingredients in a small bowl and mix until fully incorporated. Season the quails with the rub on all sides and then allow them to sit for 15 minutes.

Meanwhile, to make the glaze on the EGG, in a medium cast-iron saucepot add the olive oil and sauté the garlic, shallots, and thyme for 30 to 45 seconds, until fragrant and lightly caramelized. Add the honey and chicken broth and bring to a boil. Continue cooking for 4 to 5 minutes until slightly thickened. Remove the glaze from the EGG and set aside.

Place the quail on the EGG cooking grid and grill breast side up for 5 to 6 minutes. Flip and cook for another 5 to 6 minutes, until golden brown and cooked through. Brush the quails with glaze on both sides and cook them about 1 minute on each side, until lacquered and sticky. Repeat this process twice. Remove the quails from the EGG and serve.

Gochujang Barbecue BIG Beef Rib

Make 3 servings

Gochujang . . . say that five times fast. The spicy, sweet, and savory Korean fermented red chile paste and condiment brings a salty, spicy sweetness to the table, with a lot of depth in flavor. The English-cut short rib is a very impressive cut of meat—LARGE in size and LARGE in flavor. The barbecue sauce containing spicy gochujang, sweet molasses and brown sugar, and smoky paprika pairs oh so well with this big, bold, show-stopping short rib. I might have to change this recipe name to "MEAT LOVER"!

RUB

4 tablespoons kosher salt

1 tablespoon black pepper

1 tablespoon white pepper

1 teaspoon paprika

1 teaspoon granulated garlic

4 pounds English-cut short ribs (about 3 bones)

Apple juice, for spritzing

1 cup cherry wood chips, soaked for 1 hour in 2 cups water

SAUCE

1 cup ketchup

½ cup rice wine vinegar

3 tablespoons gochujang paste

3 tablespoons molasses

1 tablespoon light brown sugar

½ teaspoon soy sauce

1 teaspoon Worcestershire sauce

1 teaspoon smoked paprika

¼ teaspoon cayenne pepper

¼ teaspoon granulated garlic

Prepare the EGG to cook indirect with a drip pan at 300°F. To make the rub, add all of the ingredients to a small bowl and mix well. Season the short ribs thoroughly with the rub on all sides, pressing the rub into the meat. Allow the ribs to come to room temperature, about 30 to 45 minutes. Drain the wood chips and place them in the EGG over the hot coals. Place the short ribs meat side up on the EGG cooking grid and smoke for 2 hours. Spritz with apple juice after 2 hours and then continue to smoke for 2 more hours.

Meanwhile, to make the glaze on the stovetop, in a small saucepot add all of the ingredients and bring to a boil, then reduce to a simmer for 5 to 6 minutes until mixture thickens to a sauce-like consistency. Remove from the stovetop, and set aside until cooled to room temperature.

Glaze the ribs with the sauce and close the lid. After 3 minutes, glaze the ribs again and let cook for another 3 minutes. Repeat this process two more times. Remove the ribs from the EGG. Wait about 10 minutes, then slice each bone separately with a carving knife. Serve with the remaining sauce drizzled on top.

Jamaican Curry Goat Stew

Makes 6 to 8 servings

Goat is the fourth-most consumed meat in the entire world, yet many Americans have never had the pleasure of tasting it. It's extremely popular in the cuisines found in South Asia, the Middle East, Latin America, and . . . the Caribbean. It has a mild flavor and a moist texture, which make it extremely easy to blend with strong spices and sauces like curry. You won't drive too far in Jamaica without seeing a goat crossing the street, climbing a hill, or frolicking on a farm. Goat curry is a popular and readily available comfort food found in Jamaica and was a favorite in my mom's culinary arsenal growing up in a Jamaican household. The flavors of yellow Jamaican curry, garlic, thyme, and the infamous Scotch bonnet pepper are served up with rice, roti, or pita bread. You've got a Jamaican treat for the ages!

3 pounds cubed goat meat

2 tablespoons Jamaican yellow curry powder, divided

2 teaspoons kosher salt

1 teaspoon black pepper

1 teaspoon granulated onion

1 teaspoon granulated garlic

1 large yellow onion, diced

3 cloves garlic, minced

3 sprigs fresh thyme

3 green onions, white and green parts minced

1 whole Scotch bonnet pepper

¼ cup olive oil

4 cups water

1 large russet potato, large diced

Kosher salt and black pepper

Cooked rice, roti, or pita bread, for serving

In a large bowl, season the goat meat with 1 tablespoon of the curry powder and the rest of the dry ingredients. Combine the seasoned meat with the yellow onion, garlic, thyme, green onions, and pepper, and toss to combine. Place the meat in a resealable plastic bag and seal tight. Marinate it in the fridge overnight, or for at least 4 hours.

Prepare the EGG to cook indirect with a drip pan at 400°F. Remove the marinated goat meat from the fridge and allow it to come to room temperature, about 20 to 30 minutes. Place a large Dutch oven on the EGG cooking grid and add the olive oil and remaining 1 tablespoon curry powder. Add the marinated goat meat and vegetables and sear the goat on all sides for 2 to 3 minutes, until caramelized and fragrant. Cover with the water and a lid. Cook for about 1½ hours, or until tender. Add the potato and cook for 10 to 12 minutes, until the potatoes are fork tender. Season to taste with salt and pepper. Serve with rice, roti, or pita bread.

Afro-Asian Oxtails

Makes 6 servings

I'm just going to go ahead and say it: "Oxtails are my favorite food in the world!" They're very popular in Jamaican cuisine and are now finding a home in American restaurants too. Oxtails are literally the tails of cows, so they are naturally a tough meat. However, when marinated with fresh aromatics and cooked with a flavorful aromatic braising liquid and butter beans, the oxtails become luscious, sweet, and oh so tender. And as a bonus, a gravy forms. I wanted to put a twist on this Jamaican staple by acknowledging the large Asian population in Jamaica, so I included a dash of soy sauce and gochujang. I also snuck in a bit of French technique by deglazing with port wine and beef broth. Bon appétit, mon!

2 pounds oxtails, cleaned and trimmed

3 cloves garlic, peeled and smashed

1 sprig fresh thyme

2 tablespoons kosher salt

1 tablespoon black pepper

1 teaspoon granulated onion

2 teaspoons Spanish paprika

2 tablespoons light brown sugar

2 tablespoons gochujang

1 tablespoon soy sauce

4 tablespoons olive oil

1 large yellow onion, small diced

1 medium red bell pepper, seeded and small diced

1 cup port wine

32 ounces beef broth

½ cup canned butter beans, drained, not rinsed

Place the oxtails, garlic, thyme, salt, pepper, granulated onion, paprika, brown sugar, gochujang, and soy sauce in a medium bowl. Mix well until incorporated. Cover and let marinate overnight in the fridge, or for at least 4 to 5 hours.

Prepare the EGG to cook direct at 350°F. Remove the garlic and thyme from the marinade and reserve. Grill the oxtails on the EGG cooking grid for 4 to 5 minutes on each side, until browned and nicely seared. Remove from the EGG and set aside.

Place a cast-Iron Dutch oven on the EGG cooking grid and add the olive oil. Add the onions, pepper, and reserved garlic and thyme and sauté for 3 to 4 minutes, until caramelized and fragrant. Add the port wine to deglaze any bits on the bottom of the Dutch oven and cook until reduced by half. Then add the beef broth and bring to a boil. Remove the Dutch oven from the EGG.

Prepare the EGG to cook indirect with a drip pan at 350°F. Place the Dutch oven back on the EGG cooking grid. Add the oxtails back to the Dutch oven and braise for 2 to 2½ hours, until fork tender. For the last 12 to 15 minutes of cooking time, add the beans and cook until tender.

Birria Street Tacos

Makes 10 to 12 servings

What can I say about birria street tacos besides O-M-G?! That's literally the first thing I said to myself when I tasted these sinfully yummy tacos at a small but super busy Mexican taqueria in Atlanta, Georgia. In all of their cheesy, crispy, beef-dripping glory—hailing from Jalisco, Mexico—birria tacos were traditionally made with goat but are now made with beef, veal, or pork as well. These delicious bad boys are served with a side of the braising jus for dipping. I've combined the best of both worlds by using the marbleized fat found in short ribs and the intense beefy flavor of chuck roast to create a taco so good it will make your eyes roll back in your head!

1 cup pecan wood chips, soaked
   for 1 hour in 2 cups water

BIRRIA

2 pounds short ribs, flanken cut

3 pounds Angus beef chuck roast

Kosher salt and black pepper

4 cups beef broth

4 cups water

3 chipotles in adobo, seeded and
   minced, with 1 tablespoon
   adobo sauce

1 large shallot, diced

3 cloves garlic, sliced

½ cup Goya tomato-based sofrito

Vegetable oil

24 soft yellow corn tortillas

12 ounces shredded Monterey
   Jack cheese

TOPPING

1 white onion, small diced

½ cup chopped fresh cilantro

Lime wedges

Prepare the EGG to cook indirect with a drip pan at 325°F. Drain the wood chips and place them in the EGG over the hot coals. To make the birria, liberally season the short ribs and chuck roast with salt and pepper on all sides. Smoke them on the EGG cooking grid for 2 hours.

Remove the meats and increase the EGG temperature to 350°F. Place a large Dutch oven on the EGG cooking grid and add the beef broth, water, chipotles with sauce, shallot, garlic, and sofrito. Bring to a boil. Add the chuck roast and short ribs to the Dutch oven and braise for about 2 to 3 hours, until fork tender.

(continued)

(continued from page 68)

Remove the chuck roast and short ribs from the braising juices. Place the meat in a large bowl and cover with aluminum foil. Bring the braising liquid in the Dutch oven back to a gentle boil on the EGG. Leave the lid off and skim off any unwanted fat. Season to taste with salt and pepper and then remove the Dutch oven from the EGG. Remove and discard the bones from the braised meat, shred into large chunks, and toss in a large bowl with about 2 cups of the braising liquid. Season to taste, if needed, with salt and pepper.

Prepare the EGG to cook direct at 400°F. Place a cast-iron Big Green Egg *plancha* (griddle) or cast-iron pan on the EGG and add 2 tablespoons vegetable oil. Using tongs, dip both sides of the tortillas in the braising juices. Add 4 tortillas at a time to the *plancha*. Add about an ounce of cheese between 2 tortillas and a hefty spoonful of shredded meat to each of the other 2 tortillas. Cook the tortillas until golden brown and crispy. Place the beef tortilla on top of the cheese tortilla and fold over to make a taco. Repeat this process until all of the tacos are made. Be sure to wipe out and clean the *plancha* as needed between batches. Add additional vegetable oil as needed to prevent sticking or burning.

Serve the tacos with a side of warm braising liquid for dipping and top them with onion, cilantro, and lime wedges.

Porcini-Crusted Porterhouse with Sun-Dried Tomato Chimichurri

Makes 2 to 4 servings

Meat is my best friend; it's always there for me when I need it most. I find that the porterhouse is a great steak for grilling on the EGG, perfect for slicing up and sharing with family and friends. Or . . . if you're really hungry, eating it all by yourself. It's the perfect combo of New York strip and filet mignon—two steaks for the price of one. A great-quality steak doesn't need much besides salt and pepper, but I do find that a dried porcini rub adds a nice complex earthiness when the steak is grilled on the EGG. To bring it all home, I add my spin on a traditional Argentinian chimichurri with the intense sweet and tart flavor of sun-dried tomatoes. Steak . . . it's what's for dinner!

2 (24-ounce) porterhouse steaks

RUB

4 ounces dried porcini mushrooms, finely ground in a spice grinder or with a mortar and pestle

2 teaspoons granulated onion

2 teaspoons granulated garlic

2 tablespoons kosher salt

2 teaspoons black pepper

1 tablespoon granulated sugar

1 tablespoon dried oregano

CHIMICHURRI

⅓ cup minced sun-dried tomatoes

3 cloves garlic, minced

1 teaspoon chiu chow–style chili oil

1 cup olive oil

2 tablespoons sherry vinegar

½ cup finely chopped fresh Italian parsley

Kosher salt and black pepper

1 cup pecan wood chips, soaked for 1 hour in 2 cups water

(continued)

(continued from page 71)

Prepare the EGG to cook indirect with a drip pan at 225°F. Drain the wood chips and place them in the EGG over the hot coals. Pat the porterhouse steaks dry on both sides with paper towels. To make the rub, place all of the ingredients in a small bowl and whisk until well incorporated. Season the steaks liberally with the rub on both sides. Allow the steaks to come to room temperature for about 45 minutes.

Meanwhile, to make the chimichurri, combine all of the ingredients in a large bowl. Mix thoroughly and season with salt and pepper. Set aside.

Cook the porterhouse steaks on the EGG cooking grid until the filet mignon temperature reaches 10°F below your desired cooking doneness (see page 5). Remove the steaks from the EGG.

Next, prepare the EGG to cook direct at 450°F. Return the steaks to the cooking grid and sear them for about 45 seconds to 1 minute on each side. Remove the steaks from the EGG and let them rest for 8 to 9 minutes. Follow along the T-bone to remove the filet mignon and the New York strip. Slice each steak into ½ to 1-inch slices. Reassemble the sliced steak back onto the bone and serve with chimichurri on top of the steak.

Sweet and Spicy Pulled Pork

Makes 10 to 12 servings

The infamous pulled pork is the litmus test for great barbecue at any barbecue restaurant. The perfect amount of bark, rich fat, and meat is a balancing act that can take many years to perfect. However, my fail-safe recipe will give you tried-and-true awesome flavors every single time. Pork butt, rubbed down with toasty cumin, brown sugar, and a pinch of heat from the cayenne pepper that is dipped, dunked, or submerged in honey hot barbecue sauce, is for sure the way to go! Any leftovers can be used to make Pulled Pork Egg Rolls on page 29.

5 pounds bone-in pork butt

RUB
3 tablespoons kosher salt
2 teaspoons black pepper
2 teaspoons granulated garlic
2 teaspoons paprika
2 teaspoons granulated onion
2 tablespoons light brown sugar
1 teaspoon ground cumin
1 teaspoon cayenne pepper

1 cup cherry wood chips, soaked
    for 1 hour in 2 cups water

SAUCE
1 cup ketchup
¼ cup Texas Pete hot sauce
½ cup honey
½ cup apple cider vinegar
¼ cup Dijon mustard
1 tablespoon Worcestershire sauce

½ teaspoon paprika
½ teaspoon granulated garlic
½ teaspoon black pepper

1 cup apple juice

Prepare the EGG to cook indirect with a drip pan at 300°F. Rinse and pat dry the pork butt. To make the rub, place all of the ingredients in a medium bowl and whisk together. Liberally season the pork butt on all sides with the rub. Drain the wood chips and place them in the EGG over the hot coals. Place the pork butt on the EGG cooking grid and smoke for 5 to 6 hours, until the temperature reads 170°F.

Meanwhile, to make the sauce on the stovetop, in a medium-sized saucepot add all of the ingredients and bring to a boil, then reduce to a simmer. Continue to cook for 6 to 8 minutes. Remove from the stovetop and set aside.

Once the pork butt hits 170°F, remove it from the EGG. Pour the apple juice over it and then double-wrap it with butcher paper. Return the pork butt to the EGG and smoke for about another 2 hours, or until the temperature reaches 195°F. Remove it from the EGG, wrap it with a towel, and place it in a cooler until ready to pull and eat. Leftovers can be stored in the refrigerator for up to 3 days.

Korean Barbecue–Style Short Ribs

Makes 4 servings

Korean barbecue is one of those things you really have to experience for yourself. There is an open-flame grill in the middle of the table, and you are presented with a plethora of thinly sliced, well-seasoned and marinated meats and vegetables, and you grill your own dinner. That's right . . . You pay to cook your own dinner. It's such an enjoyable experience, best shared with friends and family alike. These Korean barbecue–style short ribs remind me of those days. Thinly sliced "LA-style" flanken-cut short ribs marinated in everything . . . including ginger, garlic, teriyaki sauce, sriracha, sesame oil, brown sugar: flavor, flavor, flavor. Don't walk away for too long once these are served; they tend to go pretty quickly at my barbecues!

RUB

2 tablespoons kosher salt

2 tablespoons black pepper

1 tablespoon granulated garlic

1 tablespoon smoked paprika

1 pound short ribs, sliced thin, "LA-style" flanken cut

MARINADE

1 cup teriyaki sauce

1 tablespoon sesame oil

3 tablespoons sriracha

1 cup packed dark brown sugar

¼ cup rice wine vinegar

¾ cup finely chopped green onions, green and white parts, divided

½ habanero pepper, seeded and minced

3 cloves garlic, minced

1 tablespoon peeled and freshly grated ginger root

White sesame seeds, for garnish

Prepare the EGG to cook direct at 425°F. To make the rub, place all of the ingredients in a small bowl and whisk until well incorporated. Evenly season the short ribs all over with the rub. Set aside.

To make the marinade, combine the teriyaki, sesame oil, sriracha, brown sugar, rice wine vinegar, ½ cup of the green onions, habanero, garlic, and ginger in a medium bowl and whisk until well incorporated. Place the seasoned short ribs in a large baking pan, pour the marinade over the ribs, and cover with plastic wrap. Marinate them in the fridge overnight, or for at least 3 hours.

Remove the short ribs from the fridge and bring them to room temperature for about 30 minutes. Grill the short ribs on the EGG cooking grid for 4 to 5 minutes per side, until they are nicely charred on both sides, the fat slightly crisps up, and they are cooked through. Garnish them with the remaining ¼ cup green onions and sesame seeds.

Pork Sparerib Ramen

Makes 6 to 8 servings

To say I'm obsessed with ramen is a slight understatement. Ramen broth is intense, flavorful, and layered with rich umami and a plethora of proteins that normally takes several hours to cook. Well . . . you're in luck. My recipe using the EGG will deliver all those flavors and more in under an hour. And it's Good Morning America *and* Ginger Zee *approved! Filled with brightness from the lemongrass, pungent spice from the Thai red curry paste, creaminess from the coconut milk, and meaty, tender chili-spiked spareribs and plump sweet shrimp . . . you're getting hungry . . . very hungryyyyyy.*

SPARERIBS

1½ pounds cubed cut spareribs

2 teaspoons kosher salt

1 teaspoon black pepper

1 teaspoon granulated garlic

1 teaspoon granulated onion

1 teaspoon paprika

1 tablespoon Huy Fong chili-garlic sauce or sriracha

2 tablespoons olive oil

RAMEN

3 tablespoons vegetable oil

½ medium yellow onion, small diced

3 cloves garlic, minced

2 tablespoons peeled and freshly grated ginger root

2 tablespoons minced fresh lemongrass or lemongrass paste

½ pound shiitake mushrooms, thinly sliced

6 ounces fresh spinach

Kosher salt and black pepper

2 tablespoons Thai red curry paste or gochujang

1 (13.66-ounce) can coconut milk

40 ounces chicken broth

2 teaspoons granulated sugar

1 pound shrimp (12/16 count), peeled and deveined

28 ounces cooked udon noodles, ramen noodles, angel hair, or spaghetti, cooked al dente

Bok choy, blanched for 2 minutes in salted water, and halved vertically, optional

1 cup chopped green onions, for garnish

1 cup chopped fresh cilantro, for garnish

4 medium eggs, optional

To make the spareribs, place them in a medium bowl and season with salt, pepper, granulated garlic, granulated onion, paprika, chili-garlic sauce, and the olive oil. Cover and marinate overnight, or for at least 1 hour.

Prepare the EGG to cook direct at 375°F. Grill the spareribs on the EGG cooking grid for 4 to 5 minutes on each side, until nicely browned. Remove them from the EGG.

To make the ramen, place a large Dutch oven on the EGG cooking grid and add the vegetable oil, onions, garlic, ginger, and lemongrass. Sauté for 3 to 5 minutes, until fragrant and tender. Add the mushrooms and sauté for 3 to 4 minutes, until tender. Add the spinach, a pinch of salt and pepper, and sauté for 2 to 4 minutes, until wilted. Add the curry paste and cook down for 4 to 5 minutes, until fragrant. Add the coconut milk, chicken broth, and sugar and bring to a boil. Place the spareribs in the Dutch oven, cover with a lid, and continue to cook for 22 to 25 minutes, until fork tender.

Add the shrimp to the Dutch oven and cook for 4 to 5 minutes, until plumped and fully cooked through. Season the ramen broth to taste with salt and pepper. Add a little more chili-garlic sauce or sriracha if you prefer it spicier.

To assemble each ramen bowl, place about 4 ounces of cooked noodles in the bottom of a bowl. Place the sparerib meat, shrimp, and bok choy, if using, over the noodles. Ladle some broth over the top. Garnish with green onions, fresh cilantro, or a soft-yolk egg, if using.

To make a soft-yolk egg, prepare the EGG to cook direct at 400°F. Place a saucepot on the EGG cooking grid and add 1 inch of water and bring to a boil. Carefully add the eggs to the pot, one at a time with a spoon, cover with a lid, and boil for exactly 6 minutes. After 6 minutes, remove the eggs and place them in an ice-water bath or run them under cold water. Once cool enough to handle, peel the shells and slice the eggs in half. The egg yolks should be deliciously runny.

David's "Out and In" Burger with Bacon Jam

Makes 4 servings

No trip to Los Angeles for me is complete until I make a mandatory pit stop at this landmark burger restaurant. I don't think I can mention their name, but I'm sure you can figure it out. Anyway, the sheer simplicity of the burger is what makes it so great, hot and freshly made to order with quality ingredients. This is my homage to this place and all the feels eating their burger gives me. Every burger needs a good sauce, and my tangy, sweet, and savory ketchup / mayo / mustard-based sauce isn't rocket science, but the ratio of the ingredients, and the addition of sriracha and Worcestershire sauce, gives it a nice little zip. The bacon jam is sweet with oak and chicory undernotes, as a result of cooking the bacon down with bourbon, maple syrup, brown sugar, and coffee. And American cheese, melty, lip-smacking American cheese . . . yep, my job here is done. Enjoy!

SAUCE

1 cup mayonnaise

½ cup minced bread-and-butter pickles

1 tablespoon Dijon mustard

Juice of ½ lemon

1 teaspoon paprika

1 teaspoon granulated garlic

1 teaspoon ground white pepper

1 teaspoon sriracha

½ teaspoon Worcestershire sauce

1 tablespoon ketchup

Pinch of kosher salt, to taste

JAM

8 strips bacon

2 tablespoons vegetable oil

1 cup chopped medium yellow onion

2 cloves garlic, minced

½ cup bourbon

½ cup prepared coffee

½ cup maple syrup

1 tablespoon apple cider vinegar

BURGER

2 pounds ground beef, (80% lean/20% fat)

Kosher salt and black pepper

Vegetable oil, for oiling the cooking grid

4 slices American cheese

4 hamburger buns

4 tablespoons unsalted butter, at room temperature, divided

4 romaine lettuce leaves

4 slices of beefsteak tomatoes

(continued)

(continued from page 79)

To make the sauce, place all of the ingredients in a medium bowl and mix until well incorporated. Set aside until ready to use.

Prepare the EGG to cook direct at 425°F. To make the jam, place a cast-iron pan on the EGG cooking grid and add the vegetable oil and bacon. Cook until browned and crispy, about 3 to 4 minutes on each side. Remove the bacon and place it on a paper towel–lined plate to drain and let slightly cool. Leave the bacon fat in the pan. Once the bacon is cool enough to handle, coarsely chop it and set it aside. In the pan add the onions and garlic to the bacon fat and sauté for 3 to 5 minutes, until caramelized.

Add the bourbon to the pan and reduce by half. Then add the coffee and reduce by half. Add the maple syrup, vinegar, and chopped bacon back to the pan. Bring to a boil, then continue to cook for 10 minutes, until slightly syrupy and glaze-like. Let the mixture cool slightly and then transfer to a food processor and blend until smooth. Cool the jam to room temperature before serving.

To make the burgers, form the beef into 4 equal-sized patties, about ½ inch thick. Use your thumb to create a dimple halfway into the center of each burger (this step helps reduce burger shrinkage). Season both sides of the patties liberally with salt and pepper and let rest for 10 minutes. Use the vegetable oil to oil the cooking grid to prevent the burgers from sticking. Cook the patties on the EGG cooking grid to desired doneness, ensuring a hard sear on both sides. (For medium doneness, this is about 4 minutes on each side.) Add the cheese and let it melt.

Add the Big Green Egg *plancha* to the EGG. To toast the buns, spread about ½ tablespoon butter on the cut side of each bun and place on the *plancha* for 30 to 45 seconds, until lightly toasted. For burger assembly, smear some of the sauce on the cut side of each bun. Place a patty on each bottom bun, top with jam, lettuce, and tomato, then finish with the top of each bun.

Lamb Burgers with Horseradish Mayo

Makes 4 servings

If beef is king of the burger world, I'm pretty sure that makes the lamb burger heir to the throne! My lamb burger is ba-a-a-a-d to the bone. The lamb meat provides its distinct grassy and well-balanced flavor, while the horseradish mayo gives it a nice creamy bite, and the sweet port onions provide a complexity and sweetness from the wine. Top that off with a buttery brioche bun and . . . "Fuhgedabout it!" Lights out!

MAYO

1 cup mayonnaise

1 heaping tablespoon prepared horseradish

Kosher salt and black pepper

ONIONS

1 tablespoon olive oil

1 cup finely diced yellow onion

½ cup port wine

1 tablespoon granulated sugar

BURGERS

2 pounds ground lamb meat

Kosher salt and black pepper

2 teaspoons ground cumin

Vegetable oil, for oiling the cooking grid

8 slices pepper jack cheese

4 brioche buns

4 tablespoons unsalted butter, at room temperature, divided

1½ cups arugula

To make the mayo, place the mayonnaise and horseradish in a medium bowl and whisk until well incorporated. Season to taste with salt and pepper and set aside.

Prepare the EGG to cook direct at 400°F. To make the onions, place a cast-iron pan on the EGG cooking grid and add the olive oil. Add the onions and sauté until caramelized, about 2 to 3 minutes. Add the port wine and sugar. Bring to a boil and then continue to cook for 8 to 10 minutes, until the mixture becomes slightly syrupy and the onions turn a purple hue. Remove the pan and cool the onions to room temperature.

For the burgers, form the lamb into 4 equal-sized patties, about ½ inch thick. Use your thumb to create a dimple halfway into the center of each burger (this step helps reduce burger shrinkage). Season the patties liberally with salt and pepper on both sides and lightly dust them with cumin on both sides. Let the patties rest for 10 minutes. Use the vegetable oil to oil the EGG cooking grid and grill the patties until they are golden brown and the internal temperature reaches 160°F to 165°F doneness. Melt 2 slices of cheese on each burger.

Add the Big Green Egg *plancha* to the EGG. To toast the buns, spread ½ tablespoon of butter on the cut side of each bun, and place them on the *plancha* for 30 to 45 seconds, until lightly toasted. For burger assembly, spread some mayo on the cut side of each bun. Place a patty on each bottom bun, top with some onions and arugula, then finish with the top of each bun.

Chickpea and Shiitake Mushroom Burger with Garlic Pickle Aioli and Crispy Shallots

Makes 4 servings

This is the veggie burger you've read about in fairy tales with happy endings. It's so good you won't even miss the beef. The meaty and earthy texture of the shiitakes and chickpeas provides the mouthfeel we all look for in a good, flavorful burger. It's held together with Pecorino Romano cheese and bread crumbs, which provide an additional savory note. I've added some Indian vibes to this burger with a garlic pickle aioli. What's a garlic pickle? you ask. Well, it's only a super tasty Indian condiment, bursting with flavors of cinnamon and cloves, that's mildly sweet, sour, hot, and pungent. It makes for the perfect accompaniment to this burger. And who doesn't love a crispy shallot? Crunch is texture, and texture is flavor!

BURGERS

3½ ounces shiitake mushrooms, sliced

1 cup chopped medium yellow onion

2 cloves garlic

3 tablespoons olive oil, divided

1 tablespoon kosher salt

1 tablespoon black pepper

1 cup chickpeas, drained, not rinsed

½ cup finely grated Pecorino Romano cheese

1 large egg

⅓ cup Italian-style bread crumbs

2 tablespoons canola oil

4 slices provolone cheese

4 whole-grain wheat or brioche buns

4 tablespoons unsalted butter

2 cups arugula

AIOLI

1 cup mayonnaise

1½ tablespoons Indian-style bottled garlic pickle

Juice of ½ lemon

Kosher salt

SHALLOTS

½ cup all-purpose flour

1 teaspoon kosher salt

1 teaspoon black pepper

1 teaspoon granulated garlic

1 teaspoon paprika

½ cup buttermilk

1 cup thinly sliced shallots

Canola oil, for frying

Using a sharp knife, trim off some of the excess hard fat from the brisket but leave the fat cap intact. To make the brine, place a large pot on the stovetop and add all of the ingredients. Bring the mixture to a boil. Remove the pot from the stovetop and add the ice to the brine. Allow it to cool completely, then pour it into a 13 by 19-inch baking pan that is 4 inches deep. Place the brisket fat side up in the brine and cover the pan with plastic wrap. Allow the brisket to soak in the brine for 24 hours in the refrigerator, flipping it onto the other side after the first 12 hours.

Remove the brisket from the brine after 24 hours and pat completely dry. To make the rub, in a medium bowl, combine all of the ingredients and whisk together until well incorporated. Season the brisket liberally with the rub on both sides and then place it in a clean, dry 13 by 19-inch baking pan that is 4 inches deep. Put the uncovered, rubbed brisket, fat cap side up, back into the fridge overnight, or for at least 6 to 8 hours.

Prepare the EGG to cook indirect with a drip pan at 250°F. Drain the wood chips and place them in the EGG over the hot coals. Place the brisket, fat cap side down, on the EGG cooking grid and smoke it for 5 to 6 hours (about 1 hour 15 minutes of smoking time per pound of brisket).

Remove the brisket from the EGG when the internal temperature reaches 160°F to 170°F. The brisket won't go past this temperature range at this point in the cooking process; this is called "the stall." Double-wrap the brisket in butcher paper. Place back on the EGG, fat cap side up, for 3 to 4 additional hours, until the internal temperature reaches 200°F to 205°F.

When the brisket reaches temperature, remove it from the EGG, wrap it in clean towels, and allow it to rest in an ice chest or cooler for at least 1 to 2 hours. Resting the meat allows the juices to redistribute and results in a more moist and tender brisket. The ice chest acts as a thermos and retains the heat. Slice the brisket into ¼-inch slices with an electric carving knife or sharp carving knife.

Smoked Tomahawk Prime Rib with Chanterelle Butter

Makes 12 to 14 servings

The crown jewel of any holiday, or special occasion at the dining room table, the tomahawk prime rib roast is second to none. In my opinion it deserves its own red carpet and entrance theme song when it enters the room and is presented at the dinner table. The chanterelle butter is what truly sets this tomahawk prime rib apart. It gives a peppery, earthy, and lightly fruity taste to the prime rib roast. If you can't find fresh chanterelles, feel free to substitute rehydrated dried chanterelles, or crimini mushrooms can stand in, in a pinch. This prime rib was enjoyed by all at the 2019 San Diego EGGfest. In this instance EGGin' is believin'!

BUTTER

2 tablespoons extra-virgin olive oil

2 large shallots, minced

3 cloves garlic, minced

8 ounces sliced chanterelles

Pinch of kosher salt and black pepper

1 pound unsalted butter, at room temperature

2 tablespoons chopped fresh Italian flat leaf parsley

1 (8-pound) tomahawk prime rib

Kosher salt and black pepper

Prepare the EGG to cook direct at 400°F. To make the butter, place a medium cast-iron saucepot on the EGG cooking grid and add the olive oil. Add the shallots and garlic and sauté for 2 to 3 minutes, until fragrant and lightly caramelized. Add the chanterelles to the pan, along with a pinch of salt and pepper. Continue to sauté for 6 to 8 minutes, until tender and cooked through; season to taste with salt and pepper and remove the pan from the EGG.

Cool the mushroom and shallot mixture. Once cool, add it to a food processor, along with the butter, parsley, and a pinch of salt and pepper. Blend until well incorporated and season to taste. Store the butter in the fridge until ready to use, then bring it to room temperature.

Prepare the EGG to cook indirect with a drip pan at 350°F. Generously season the prime rib with salt and pepper on all sides. Allow it to come to room temperature for about 2 to 3 hours, depending on how big it is. Rub the prime rib all over with two-thirds of the butter. Reserve about one-third of the butter to slather with at the end.

Place the prime rib in the center of the EGG cooking grid, fat cap side up, and insert a meat probe or EGG Genius probe in the thickest center part of the prime rib. Cook it for about 2 hours, or until the internal temperature reads 120°F (for medium-rare doneness). The rule of thumb is about 15 minutes of cooking time per pound; keep in mind the prime rib will continue to cook 5°F to 10°F more when taken off the EGG.

When done, remove the prime rib from the EGG and slather it all over with the remaining third of the butter. Tent it with aluminum foil and allow it to rest for about 30 minutes. Once the prime rib has rested, slice it to desired thickness and portion sizes. Serve a portion of the butter on the side and/or Alabama White Barbecue Sauce (page 19).

CHAPTER

5

UNDER THE SEA

(SEAFOOD)

Man shall not live by meat alone . . . especially when there are oceans and lakes around, with such delightful seafood to devour. The plethora of different seafood options and preparations is limitless, and you can cook them all on the Big Green Egg. These recipes are structured in a way so you can apply the various cooking applications, seasonings, sauces, and preparations to other seafood varieties as well. Seafood has a naturally sweet and briny taste to it, so I really highlight and accentuate those flavors while helping retain that moisture. Okay . . . so this is the part where you cook!

Saffron PEI Mussels

Makes 4 to 6 servings

Everybody loves muscles and mussels . . . And if you don't like mussels, you just haven't had mine yet. The sweet brininess of mussels is always a welcomed treat at my dining room table. The warm spice and distinct flavor of Spanish saffron open up the door of alluring aroma and say: "Hey, come on in! We've been waiting for you." The salty and savory pancetta adds just the right amount of fat to the dish, and the sofrito really hones in on those Spanish flavors. Toast up some sourdough bread on the EGG and get ready to sop up all that seafood brothy goodness!

3 tablespoons olive oil

¼ pound pancetta, small diced

2 whole large shallots, minced

3 cloves garlic, minced

1 teaspoon saffron threads

3 tablespoons Goya tomato-based sofrito

Pinch of kosher salt and black pepper

¾ cup white wine

2 pounds PEI mussels, cleaned, scrubbed, and debearded

4 tablespoons unsalted butter

¼ cup chopped fresh Italian flat leaf parsley

GRILLED SOURDOUGH

6 slices sourdough bread

Olive oil, for grilling the bread

Kosher salt and black pepper

Prepare the EGG to cook direct with the wok setup at 425°F. Add the olive oil and pancetta and sauté for 3 to 4 minutes, until browned. Add the shallots and garlic and constantly sauté for 1 to 2 minutes, until lightly caramelized. Add the saffron, sofrito, and pinch of salt and pepper and sauté for an additional minute. Then add the wine and mussels and close the EGG for 3 to 4 minutes, until the wine reduces by half and the mussels open up. Remove the wok from the EGG, add the butter and parsley, and swirl the wok until the pan sauce emulsifies. Season to taste with salt and pepper.

For the grilled sourdough, lightly drizzle each slice of bread with about a tablespoon of olive oil and lightly season with salt and pepper on both sides. Grill the bread directly on the EGG cooking grid for about 1 minute per side, or until crisped and golden brown. Serve with the mussels.

Harissa Prawns

Makes 4 servings

There's nothing more satisfying than getting messy while devouring head-on prawns dripping with a rich and tasty sauce. It's not gonna be the prettiest thing to watch me eat, but I guarantee it's gonna be delicious. These are sautéed with berbere spice (a tantalizing Ethiopian spice blend) and harissa paste (a Tunisian hot chili pepper paste) and mellowed out with tomato paste. Finish with butter and pair with toasty-crusty fresh sourdough bread. That's all I have to say about that. (One small suggestion . . . I wouldn't wear any white clothing while eating this . . . speaking from experience.)

3 tablespoons olive oil

1 pound prawns (U12 count), washed, cleaned, and deveined, head and shell on (you can remove the shells, but keeping them on adds more flavor)

2 whole medium shallots, minced

2 cloves garlic, minced

1 green onion, green and white parts finely minced, plus more for garnish

¼ teaspoon berbere spice

Pinch of kosher salt and black pepper

2 tablespoons harissa paste

1 tablespoon tomato paste

1 cup chicken broth

5 tablespoons unsalted butter

1 tablespoon chopped fresh Italian flat leaf parsley

1 tablespoon chopped fresh cilantro

GRILLED SOURDOUGH

4 slices sourdough bread

Olive oil, for grilling the bread

Kosher salt and black pepper

Prepare the EGG to cook direct at 425°F. Place a 12-inch cast-iron pan on the EGG cooking grid and add the olive oil. Add the prawns and get a nice sear on both sides. The prawns will start to change color after 2 to 3 minutes on each side. Then add the shallots, garlic, and green onions and sauté for 30 seconds. Add the berbere spice and salt and pepper, sautéing constantly. Add the harissa paste and tomato paste and continue to sauté for about 1 minute. Add the chicken broth, close the EGG, and let the prawns cook for 2 to 3 minutes more, until tender and cooked through. Add the butter, parsley, and cilantro and sauté for another minute, until the butter emulsifies into a pan sauce. Remove the pan immediately from the EGG, before the sauce breaks. Season to taste with salt and pepper and garnish with sliced green onions.

For the grilled sourdough, lightly drizzle each slice of bread with about a tablespoon of olive oil and lightly season with salt and pepper on both sides. Grill the bread directly on the EGG cooking grid for about 1 minute per side, or until crisped and golden brown. Serve with the prawns.

Grilled Garlicky Lobster Tails

Makes 8 servings

Lobster tails are an easy, fast, and classy way to add surf to any turf. They have a natural sweetness and salinity to them that make them perfect for grilling on the EGG. Lobster tails and melted butter go together like peas and carrots or, better yet, Thelma and Louise! So I've taken the liberty of taking care of that step for you already, by brushing them with a garlicky butter to give them a hint of smokiness from smoked paprika. You can grill up these lobster tails on the EGG in no time and impress any guest.

GARLIC BUTTER

4 ounces unsalted butter, melted

1 teaspoon kosher salt

½ teaspoon white pepper

½ teaspoon smoked paprika

2 cloves garlic, minced

2 tablespoons chopped fresh Italian
flat leaf parsley

Vegetable oil, for oiling the cooking grid

4 raw lobster tails, split in half,
keep shell on

Prepare the EGG to cook direct at 400°F. To make the garlic butter, place all of the ingredients in a small bowl and whisk until incorporated. Set aside.

Oil the EGG cooking grid with the vegetable oil. Brush the garlic butter on the lobster tails and then place them on the EGG, meat side down. After 5 minutes flip the lobster tails meat side up and brush again with garlic butter. Continue to cook them for about another 3 minutes and remove them when they're golden brown. Brush them with the garlic butter once more and serve.

Za'atar Grilled Salmon Steaks with Cashew Relish

Makes 2 Servings

Besides the word "za'atar" being fun to say, it's also a delicious Middle Eastern spice blend consisting primarily of sesame seeds, dried sumac, salt, and other spices. This rub goes very well with steak-like fish that can handle a bit of an aggressive and bold seasoning. Swordfish and mahi-mahi would work great for this recipe as well. Grilled to perfection on the EGG, the fish is topped with a bright and fresh cashew relish. The creamy cashews, the hint of heat from the jalapeño, and the fresh vegetables really give the fish a clean finish that cuts through the fattiness of the salmon. Za'atARE you excited yet (slow eye wink)?

2 (½-pound, 2-inch-thick) Scottish
  salmon steaks, skin on

RUB
2 tablespoons za'atar spice blend
1 teaspoon kosher salt
1 teaspoon smoked paprika
1 teaspoon black pepper
½ teaspoon granulated garlic
2 tablespoons olive oil

RELISH
1 cup coarsely chopped salted,
  roasted cashews
½ cup chopped fresh cilantro
2 tablespoons minced jalapeño, seeded
2 tablespoons minced shallots
½ cup rice wine vinegar
2 tablespoons honey
Kosher salt and black pepper

Prepare the EGG to cook direct at 400°F. To make the rub, place all of the ingredients in a small bowl and mix until fully incorporated. Generously season both sides of the salmon steaks with the rub. Grill the salmon on the EGG cooking grid for 6 to 8 minutes per side (for medium doneness) or more, depending on desired doneness and crispness of the salmon skin.

Meanwhile, to make the relish, combine all of the ingredients in a small bowl. Season to taste with salt and pepper. Set aside.

Remove the salmon steaks from the EGG, top with the relish, and serve.

Southern Shrimp 'n' Grits

Makes 4 servings

This shrimp 'n' grits recipe is what shook the world up into a frenzy in the summer of 2017 when Iron Chef *and* Food Network *personality Bobby Flay and I faced off in a shrimp 'n' grits showdown when I competed as a finalist on* Food Network Star, *season 13. Being a chef and living in the South for almost twenty years, you could say I knew more than a little bit about shrimp 'n' grits. I've cooked them, oh . . . at least two hundred times. This dish isn't lacking in flavor or spice, with a decadent Cajun andouille cream sauce atop dry-rubbed, perfectly grilled shrimp and creamy grits built with chicken broth, heavy cream, and a substantial amount of Parmesan cheese. This is a dish great for brunch, breakfast, dinner, or a late-night snack—heck, anytime! It really gives your appetite a warm embrace.*

SHRIMP

1 pound jumbo shrimp (10/15 count), peeled and deveined

1 teaspoon kosher salt

1 teaspoon black pepper

2 teaspoons paprika

¼ teaspoon cayenne pepper

1 teaspoon granulated garlic

1 tablespoon olive oil

SAUCE

1 tablespoon unsalted butter

2 tablespoons olive oil

½ cup small-diced medium yellow onion

½ cup small-diced medium red bell pepper

1 tablespoon minced garlic

5 to 6 ounces andouille sausage (about 1 large andouille sausage link), small diced

¼ teaspoon cayenne pepper

½ teaspoon paprika

¼ teaspoon granulated garlic

¼ teaspoon black pepper

1 cup heavy cream

Kosher salt and black pepper

¼ cup chopped fresh Italian flat leaf parsley

GRITS

2½ cups chicken broth

½ teaspoon salt

½ teaspoon granulated garlic

½ cup yellow grits

½ cup heavy cream

4 ounces freshly grated Parmesan cheese

Kosher salt and black pepper

Prepare the EGG to cook direct at 375°F. To make the shrimp, place it with the seasonings and olive oil in a medium bowl and thoroughly mix. Set aside.

To make the sauce, add the butter and olive oil to a medium cast-iron saucepot on the EGG cooking grid. Add the onion and pepper and sauté for about 2 to 3 minutes, or until caramelized. Add the sausage, cayenne pepper, paprika, granulated garlic, and black pepper and sauté for about 5 minutes, until the sausage is cooked through and brown. Add the heavy cream and bring to a boil. Then continue to cook the mixture for 3 to 5 minutes, until it thickens and reaches a sauce-like consistency. Season to taste with salt and pepper. Stir in the parsley to finish.

Meanwhile, to make the grits, place a medium cast-iron saucepot on the EGG cooking grid and add the chicken broth, salt, and granulated garlic. Bring to a boil. Whisk in the grits, cover the pot with a lid, and move it to a cooler spot on the EGG. Cook for 6 to 8 minutes, until the grits become tender and smooth. Whisk in the heavy cream and cheese and continue to cook for another 2 to 3 minutes, until the grits are luscious and creamy. Season to taste with salt and pepper.

Place the shrimp on the EGG cooking grid and grill for 4 to 5 minutes per side, until cooked through and slightly charred.

For assembly, place the grits on the plate, top with shrimp, and finish with some sauce.

Grilled Asian Prawns with Almond Satay Sauce and Mango Salsa

Makes 6 servings

Hello, Southeast Asia, did you miss me? This prawn recipe checks so many boxes for me. First, we're in China, with the warm spices found in Chinese five spice: star anise, cloves, Chinese cinnamon, Szechuan peppercorns, and fennel seeds. Then we're heading on over to Indonesia, where we have the satay to get the partay going. Traditionally, satay is a skewered grilled meat or seafood served with a sauce. Here creamy coconut milk is infused with Thai red curry paste, almond butter, and lemongrass. And last, we go to Thailand, where mango is commonly paired with curries. The salsa and satay sauce can be made the night before, so you only have to focus on grilling the prawns/shrimp when you're ready to serve.

PRAWNS

2 pounds prawns or large shrimp (10/15 count), deveined and peeled, tail on

1 tablespoon Chinese five spice

1 teaspoon kosher salt

1 teaspoon white pepper

½ teaspoon granulated garlic

½ teaspoon paprika

2 teaspoons granulated sugar

1 tablespoon olive oil

SAUCE

2 tablespoons olive oil

2 cloves garlic, minced

1 teaspoon minced lemongrass or lemongrass paste

3 tablespoons Thai red curry paste

1 (13.66-ounce) can coconut milk

1 tablespoon spicy Hunan-style stir-fry sauce

¼ cup almond butter

¼ teaspoon granulated sugar

Kosher salt and black pepper

2 tablespoons chopped fresh cilantro

SALSA

1 cup small-diced mango, fresh or frozen, thawed

¼ cup mango nectar

¼ cup small-diced yellow onion

¼ cup small-diced jalapeño, seeded

1 tablespoon chopped fresh cilantro

Juice of ½ lime

Kosher salt and black pepper

(continued)

(continued from page 99)

Prepare the EGG to cook direct at 375°F. To make the prawns, place them in a medium bowl and add all of the dry ingredients and the olive oil. Mix until well coated. Skewer the prawns with 2 parallel skewers, to keep the prawns secure.

To make the sauce, place a medium cast-iron saucepot on the cooking grid of the EGG, add the olive oil, garlic, and lemongrass and sauté for about 1 minute, or until lightly fragrant. Add the red curry paste and sauté for about 2 minutes, until nutty and fragrant. Add the coconut milk, stir-fry sauce, almond butter, and sugar and then bring to a boil. Continue to cook for about 5 to 6 minutes, until reaching a sauce-like consistency. Season to taste with salt and pepper. Finish with the fresh cilantro.

Meanwhile, to make the salsa, combine all of the ingredients in a small bowl. Season to taste with salt and pepper. Set aside.

Grill the prawns on the EGG cooking grid for 4 to 5 minutes per side, until golden brown and cooked through. Serve with the sauce and salsa.

Salt & Pepper Shrimp

Makes 4 servings

Salt-N-Pepa wasn't only a hit '80s rap group but is also an amazingly quick, simple, and flavorful shrimp preparation. Look no further than your local Chinese restaurant and chances are you will find salt-and-pepper shrimp on their menu. This recipe is a great way to utilize the EGG wok, and it's pretty quick to whip up. Tossing the shrimp with cornstarch and rice flour ensures crunchy shrimp, before tossing them with kosher salt and pepper. I like to include a bit of freshness with wok-fried jalapeños, shallots, garlic, and ginger. You might want to double—wait, no, triple—this recipe. Because I'm sure your guests will want seconds!

¼ cup cornstarch

¼ cup rice flour

3 cups plus 1 tablespoon vegetable oil, divided

1 pound shrimp (21/25 count), peeled and deveined, tail on

1 small jalapeño, seeded and thinly sliced

¼ cup shallots, thinly sliced

1 tablespoon peeled and freshly minced ginger root

3 cloves garlic, thinly sliced

1 teaspoon kosher salt

1 teaspoon black pepper

2 tablespoons chopped fresh cilantro, for garnish

2 tablespoons green onions, white and green parts minced, for garnish

Prepare the EGG to cook direct with the wok setup at 425°F. Place the cornstarch and rice flour in a medium bowl and whisk until incorporated. Set aside.

Add 3 cups of the oil to the wok and wait for the temperature to reach 350°F to 375°F. Check whether the oil is ready by dropping a little cornstarch in to see if it sizzles. Toss the shrimp in the cornstarch mixture and shake off any excess. Add the shrimp and fry in batches of 6 for 2 to 3 minutes, flipping midway through cooking, until crispy and cooked through. Place the finished shrimp on a wire rack set over a paper towel–lined sheet pan to drain. Continue until all of the shrimp are fried.

Clean and dry the wok. Place it back on the EGG and add the remaining 1 tablespoon oil, jalapeño, shallot, ginger, and garlic. Constantly stir-fry for 35 to 40 seconds, until fragrant and lightly caramelized. While stir-frying, place the shrimp back in the wok with the salt and pepper. Continue to consistently stir-fry for about 15 to 20 seconds, until well incorporated. Garnish with cilantro and green onions.

Jumbo Lump Crab Cakes with Pomegranate Vinaigrette

Makes 2 servings

This jumbo lump crab cake recipe is near and dear to my heart because it's requested pretty often by family and friends. The secret formula . . . let the jumbo lump crabmeat shine like the star it is. I use very little filler, just enough to help it bind. The Ritz crackers give the crab cakes a nice crunch and a buttery flavor, while the Old Bay seasoning truly accentuates those beautiful natural flavors of the crab.

VINAIGRETTE

¾ cup extra-virgin olive oil

¼ cup rice wine vinegar

½ cup pomegranate juice

Juice of ½ lemon

¼ cup honey

2 teaspoons Dijon mustard

Kosher salt and black pepper

CRAB CAKES

½ cup mayonnaise

2 teaspoons whole-grain Dijon mustard

2 dashes of hot sauce

2 teaspoons Old Bay seasoning

½ teaspoon white pepper

¼ teaspoon granulated garlic

Juice of ½ lemon

1 pound jumbo lump crabmeat

30 Ritz crackers, finely blended in a food processor, divided

2 tablespoons canola oil

2 tablespoons unsalted butter

8 ounces baby mixed greens

Prepare the EGG to cook direct with a Big Green Egg *plancha* at 400°F. To make the vinaigrette, place all of the ingredients in a medium bowl and whisk until well incorporated. Season to taste with salt and pepper and set aside.

To make the crab cakes, add the mayonnaise, mustard, hot sauce, Old Bay, pepper, granulated garlic, and lemon juice to a medium bowl and whisk to combine. Gently fold in the crabmeat, then gently fold in the cracker crumbs. Carefully form the mixture into medium-sized crab cakes, about ½ inch thick. Place in the fridge for about 15 minutes to allow the crab cakes to firm up.

Add the oil and butter to the *plancha*. When the butter is melted, add the crab cakes and cook for 4 to 5 minutes per side, until golden brown and warmed throughout.

Toss the mixed greens with the vinaigrette and serve topped with the crab cakes.

Blackened Diver Scallops with Crawfish Étouffée

Makes 5 servings

I like to describe a nice big, plump diver scallop as the "filet mignon" of the ocean. It's delicate, meaty, sweet, and mild, and it really pairs well with a wide array of flavors. This makes it an exceptional choice to lightly blacken on the EGG and serve with a crawfish étouffée sauce. A truly Cajun-inspired dish, with the Cajun seasoning and the moderately spiced crawfish étouffée, it's a New Orleans favorite, chock-full of crawfish, the holy trinity (onions, celery, and bell pepper), and a rich, savory tomato sauce, thickened with a blond roux. Laissez le bon temps rouler (Let the good times roll)!

SEASONING

1 tablespoon kosher salt

1½ teaspoons paprika

¾ teaspoon black pepper

¾ teaspoon granulated garlic

¾ teaspoon granulated onion

1½ teaspoons dried thyme leaves

¾ teaspoon cayenne pepper

ÉTOUFFÉE

4 tablespoons olive oil

2 tablespoons unsalted butter

1 small yellow onion, small diced

1 medium red bell pepper, seeded and small diced

2 stalks celery, small diced

2 cloves garlic, minced

½ cup tomato sauce

2½ tablespoons all-purpose flour

3 cups chicken broth

1 pound Louisiana crawfish tail meat

Kosher salt and black pepper

SCALLOPS

10 large diver scallops, cleaned, abductor muscle removed

3 tablespoons olive oil

2 tablespoons unsalted butter

Juice of ½ lemon

(continued)

(continued from page 103)

Prepare the EGG to cook direct at 400°F. To make the seasoning, place all of the ingredients in a small bowl and whisk until incorporated. Set aside.

To make the étouffée, place a large cast-iron pan on the cooking grid of the EGG, add the olive oil and butter. Add the onions, peppers, celery, and garlic and sauté for 3 to 4 minutes, until caramelized. Add the tomato sauce and 1 teaspoon of the seasoning to the pan and sauté for an additional 2 to 3 minutes. Add the flour and continuously stir for about 2 to 3 minutes, until the flour dissolves into the veggies. Add the chicken broth, whisk all of the ingredients until well incorporated, and bring to a boil. Continue to cook for 6 to 8 minutes, until thickened.

Add the crawfish tail meat and 1 teaspoon of the seasoning and return to a boil, continually stirring.

Continue to cook for about 5 to 6 minutes, or until the crawfish plump up. Season to taste with salt and pepper.

Pat the scallops dry on both sides with paper towels. Season them on both sides liberally with seasoning. Place a large cast-iron pan on the EGG cooking grid and add the olive oil. Add the scallops to the pan and get a hard sear on them, about 3 to 4 minutes. Add the butter and lemon juice to the pan and swirl until the butter is melted. Flip the scallops and baste them with the lemon butter. Allow the scallops to cook undisturbed for another 2 to 3 minutes. Serve immediately with the hot étouffée.

CHAPTER

6

BREAKIN' THE FAST

(BREAKFAST)

The best part of waking up is . . . BREAKFAST! (Sorry, coffee . . .) Breakin' the fast! You have slept, snored, and dreamed the night away. What's the first thing you do when you wake up in the morning? Make a hearty and delicious meal everybody can enjoy. Breakfast is one of my favorite meals of the day, and it runs the gamut from savory to sweet to every flavor in between. The multifunctional EGG is the key to the success of all of these breakfast recipes. From banana-nut pancakes griddled on the plancha to a Southern breakfast quiche inspired by the Cajun flavors of the South, you will never look at breakfast the same again. So hurry up and go to bed, so you can wake up and break the fast on the EGG!

Southern Breakfast Quiche

Makes 8 servings

Probably one of the first "fancy" breakfast items I made as a teenager was a quiche. And, boy, was I proud of it. This southern-inspired quiche can be enjoyed hot or at room temperature. Stuffed with andouille sausage, shrimp, mushrooms, spinach, and cheddar cheese. Why can't brunch be every day?

SHRIMP

½ pound shrimp (21/25 count), peeled and deveined

¼ teaspoon kosher salt

¼ teaspoon black pepper

¼ teaspoon smoked paprika

¼ teaspoon granulated garlic

QUICHE

2 tablespoons olive oil

¼ pound andouille sausage (about 1 link), small diced

¼ medium yellow onion, minced

2 cloves garlic, minced

1 cup thinly sliced baby portobello (or crimini) mushrooms

1 cup coarsely chopped spinach

1 (9-inch) frozen prepared pie crust

6 large eggs

½ cup heavy cream

½ teaspoon kosher salt

¼ teaspoon black pepper

¼ teaspoon hot sauce

½ cup shredded sharp cheddar cheese

EGG WASH

1 medium egg

2 teaspoons water

Prepare the EGG to cook direct at 425°F. To make the shrimp, place it and the spices in a small bowl and toss well. Set aside.

To make the quiche, place a large cast-iron pan on the EGG cooking grid and add the oil. Add the sausage and cook for 4 to 5 minutes, until browned and cooked through. Remove the sausage from the pan and reserve the fat in the pan. Add the onion and garlic and sauté for about 1 minute, or until fragrant. Add the mushrooms and sauté for 2 to 3 minutes, until soft. Add the spinach and sauté for about 1 minute. Then add the shrimp and sauté for 3 to 4 minutes, until slightly browned. Remove the pan from the EGG, place the contents in a bowl, and cool to room temperature.

Prepare the EGG to cook indirect with a drip pan at 425°F. Use a fork to prick the bottom of the crust. In a large bowl, whisk the eggs, heavy cream, salt and pepper, and hot sauce, until well incorporated. Spread the sautéed vegetables, shrimp, and sausage evenly on the bottom of the pie crust and top with the cheese. Pour the egg mixture over the contents.

In a small bowl, whisk together the egg and water until blended and brush the pie crust with the egg wash. Bake the quiche in the EGG for 30 to 35 minutes, until cooked through and a toothpick comes out clean.

Deep-Dish Breakfast Hash Browns

Makes 6 servings

They're crispy, they're soft, they're salty, and they're cheesy; they have everything you love in hash browns and more: thick hash brown patties stuffed with bacon, sharp cheddar cheese, and green onions, all topped with a cheese fondue and chive sour cream. These are the loaded baked potatoes of hash browns . . . and I'm completely fine with that.

HASH BROWNS

8 bacon lardons, sliced in 1-inch pieces, divided

4 cups frozen hash browns

Kosher salt and black pepper

1 teaspoon granulated garlic

1 teaspoon granulated onion

2 tablespoons dehydrated potato flakes or panko bread crumbs

1 cup freshly shredded cheddar cheese

1 large egg, beaten

2 tablespoons canola oil

½ cup chopped green onions, white and green parts

SOUR CREAM

8 ounces sour cream

2 tablespoons chopped fresh chives

¼ teaspoon kosher salt

½ teaspoon granulated onion

½ teaspoon granulated garlic

Juice from ½ lemon

Kosher salt and black pepper

FONDUE

1 tablespoon unsalted butter

1 tablespoon all-purpose flour

1 cup heavy cream

¼ teaspoon granulated garlic

1½ cups freshly shredded sharp cheddar cheese

Kosher salt and black pepper

Prepare the EGG to cook direct at 400°F. To make the hash browns, place a large cast-iron pan on the EGG cooking grid and add the bacon lardons. Cook for 4 to 6 minutes, until browned and the fat has rendered. Remove the bacon from the pan using a slotted spoon and drain on a paper towel–lined plate. Reserve the bacon fat in the pan and sauté the shredded hash browns for 5 to 6 minutes, until cooked and tender. Season to taste with salt and pepper. Remove the pan from the heat and transfer the hash browns to a medium bowl to cool for 5 to 6 minutes.

Add the granulated garlic, granulated onion, half of the bacon lardons, potato flakes, and cheese to the hash browns. Mix until well incorporated. Add salt and pepper to taste. Add the egg and mix until thoroughly combined. Divide the hash brown mix into 3 to 4 baseball-sized balls and shape to 1½-inch-thick rectangular patties.

To make the sour cream, combine all of the ingredients in a medium bowl and whisk until well incorporated. Season to taste with salt and pepper and set aside.

Place a clean cast-iron pan on the cooking grid of the EGG, and add the canola oil. Panfry the formed hash brown patties for 3 to 5 minutes on each side, until crispy and golden brown.

Meanwhile, to make the fondue on the stovetop, in a medium-sized saucepot, melt the butter and whisk in the flour until it makes a light roux. Whisk in the heavy cream and continue to whisk as it boils and thickens. Whisk in the granulated garlic and cheese until melted and incorporated. Season to taste with salt and pepper.

To serve, top the hash browns with fondue, sour cream, green onions, and the remaining bacon lardons.

Banana-Nut Pancakes with Rum-Caramel Sauce

Makes 6 to 8 servings

It's breakfast, it's dessert . . . no, it's both. These pancakes are a creation that just popped in my head one day. I said to myself: "Self . . . what would happen if a banana-nut muffin and a pancake had a baby?" And the banana-nut pancake was born! Stuffed with bananas and walnuts and griddled on the EGG until golden brown is a great start, but where this recipe really shines is in the sauce . . . a creamy spiced rum sauce with a kick and bananas folded right in there. Give this recipe a test-drive for breakfast or even for a sweet treat after dinner. Stack 'em up and mow 'em down!

SAUCE

1½ cups spiced dark rum

2 tablespoons unsalted butter

1 cup packed light brown sugar

2 cups heavy cream

½ teaspoon kosher salt

2 ripe bananas, sliced

PANCAKES

1½ cups all-purpose flour

3 tablespoons granulated sugar

1 tablespoon light brown sugar

1 teaspoon ground cinnamon

¼ teaspoon allspice

2 teaspoons baking powder

¼ teaspoon baking soda

½ teaspoon kosher salt

1 cup milk

3 large eggs

1 teaspoon vanilla extract

1 tablespoon spiced rum

1 tablespoon unsalted butter, melted

2 tablespoons unsalted butter, or
   vegetable cooking spray

1 cup chopped walnuts

2 bananas, thinly sliced

6 ounces crushed pralines, for garnish

½ cup confectioners' sugar, for garnish

(continued)

(continued from page 112)

Prepare the EGG to cook direct with a *plancha* at 400°F. To make the sauce on the stovetop, place the rum in a large saucepot and bring to a boil. Reduce to medium heat, and continue to cook until reduced by half. Add the butter and brown sugar to the pot and whisk until well incorporated. Add the heavy cream and bring to a boil. Then add the salt. Continue to cook for 3 to 4 minutes, until the sauce thickens and reaches the consistency of caramel. Fold in the bananas and continue to simmer for about 2 minutes. Set aside. Rewarm the sauce when ready to serve on the pancakes.

To make the pancakes, whisk together the dry ingredients in a large bowl. Whisk together the milk, eggs, vanilla, rum, and melted butter in a separate medium bowl. Make a well in the middle of the dry ingredients. Gradually whisk the wet ingredients into the well in the dry ingredients, until well incorporated and the batter is smooth.

Add the butter or cooking spray to the Big Green Egg *plancha*. Pour the batter into 4 to 5-inch-diameter circles and place about 1 tablespoon of walnuts and 3 to 4 banana slices on top of each pancake. Cook the pancakes until bubbles begin to form, use a slotted steel spatula to look under the pancake, and flip them once golden brown. Continue to cook the pancakes for 3 to 5 minutes, until cooked through. Repeat until you've used the remaining batter. Serve topped with the sauce, pralines, and powdered sugar.

Savory Breakfast Bread Pudding

Makes 8 to 10 servings

Why should dessert bread pudding have all the fun? Allow me to introduce everybody to my savory breakfast bread pudding. It includes everything that a great breakfast should have: breakfast sausage, eggs, cheese, and croissants . . . Say whatttttt?! This custardy bread pudding is my whimsical reimagining of breakfast, but feel free to make it yours; this is simply a blueprint to the deliciousness. Now go forth and prosper . . . and pair this with Southern–Style White Sausage Gravy (page 117) too.

2 tablespoons unsalted butter, divided

1 pound ground breakfast sausage

1 medium yellow onion, finely minced

3 cloves garlic, minced

1 teaspoon ground thyme

½ teaspoon crushed red pepper, optional

1 tablespoon olive oil

8 ounces thinly sliced baby portobello (or crimini) mushrooms

Pinch of kosher salt

1 cup chicken broth

½ loaf (about 9 slices) white sandwich bread, crust removed and cut into 1-inch pieces

3 large croissants, cut into 1-inch pieces

1½ cups shredded sharp cheddar cheese

1½ cups shredded Parmesan cheese, divided

¾ cup chopped fresh Italian flat leaf parsley (reserve ¼ cup for garnish)

6 large eggs

2 cups heavy cream

1 teaspoon kosher salt

½ teaspoon black pepper

(continued)

(continued from page 115)

Prepare the EGG to cook direct at 375°F. Grease a 9 by 13-inch EGG-safe baking pan or dish with 1 tablespoon of the butter. Place a cast-iron pan on the cooking grid of the EGG, add the remaining 1 tablespoon butter, and cook the sausage for 8 to 10 minutes, until cooked through and browned. Break apart the sausage in the pan. Use a slotted spoon to remove the cooked sausage and cool to room temperature, retaining the fat in the pan.

Add the onion, garlic, thyme, and crushed red pepper, if using, to the pan; sauté for 2 to 3 minutes, until slightly browned. Add the olive oil, mushrooms, and salt. Sauté the mushrooms for 5 to 7 minutes, until cooked, tender, and caramelized. Add the chicken broth and reduce to a quarter of its original volume. Remove the pan from the EGG and cool the mushroom mixture to room temperature.

Add the bread, croissants, mushrooms, sausage, sharp cheddar, 1 cup of the Parmesan, and ½ cup parsley to a large bowl. Fold everything together with a rubber spatula. Once everything is incorporated, pour the contents into the prepared 9 by 13-inch pan. In a separate large bowl, whisk together the eggs, heavy cream, salt, and pepper until well mixed. Pour the mixture evenly over the contents of the pan, spread everything out evenly, and smooth the surface with a rubber spatula. Cover the pan with plastic wrap and place it in the fridge for 2 to 3 hours, to allow the flavors to set. Remove the pan from the refrigerator and use the remaining ½ cup Parmesan to top the bread pudding.

Prepare the EGG to cook indirect at 375°F. Bake in the EGG for 45 minutes to 1 hour, until puffed up, golden brown, cooked through, and caramelized. Serve immediately, topped with remaining parsley, grated Parmesan cheese, and a side of Southern–Style White Sausage Gravy (page 117).

Note: To make a vegetarian savory bread pudding, substitute plant-based sausage and replace the chicken broth with vegetable broth.

Southern–Style White Sausage Gravy

Makes 6 to 8 servings

Serve this simple and tasty white sausage gravy with my Savory Breakfast Bread Pudding (page 115) or with biscuits, toast, grits, or an omelet. It really reflects a bit of the South I've grown to love, since relocating to Atlanta. A savory white gravy, with caramelized sweet Vidalia onions, is ready to answer all of your breakfast needs. Or smother it on chicken or pork chops for brunch . . . Can't forget those!

2 tablespoons unsalted butter

¾ cup spicy pork sausage, removed from casings

2 cloves garlic, minced

½ cup Vidalia onion, medium diced

2 tablespoons all-purpose flour

¼ cup half-and-half

½ cup heavy cream

Kosher salt and black pepper

Prepare the EGG to cook direct at 375°F. Place a medium cast-iron skillet on the EGG cooking grid and heat the butter. Add the sausage and using a wooden spoon break up any large pieces. Cook for 6 minutes, until browned. Use a slotted spoon to remove the sausage to a plate and set aside; do not line the plate with paper towels.

In the same pan, add the garlic and onion. Cook for 2 to 3 minutes, until tender. Whisk in the flour and add the half-and-half and heavy cream. Whisk to combine. Cook, stirring, until the mixture is thickened and coats the back of a spoon. Return the sausage to the gravy, and stir until well incorporated. Season to taste with salt and pepper.

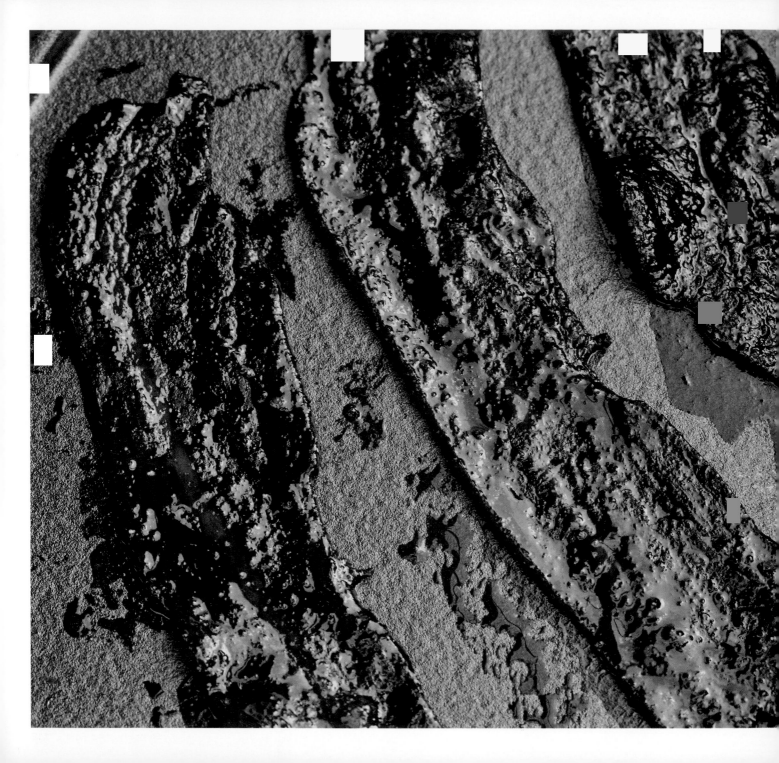

Kick'd Up Bacon Candy

Makes 10 servings

I can literally just walk around all day snacking on this bacon candy. It's the quintessential perfect balance of sweet and spicy. Lacquered sticky bacon, glistening with sweet maple syrup, black pepper, and cayenne pepper . . . take one bite and you'll see why I describe this as "kick'd up." It's great for breakfast or even to hand out to trick-or-treaters for Halloween. Seriously, I would gladly take this treat!

10 slices thick-cut bacon

1 cup maple syrup

1 tablespoon light brown sugar

1 teaspoon black pepper

¼ teaspoon cayenne pepper

Prepare the EGG to cook indirect at 375°F. Place the EGGspander in the EGG and a drip pan underneath the top grate. Place the bacon on the top rack of the EGGspander, right over the drip pan. After 18 to 20 minutes, flip the bacon and continue cooking until slightly brown.

Meanwhile, in a medium bowl, whisk together the maple syrup, brown sugar, black pepper, and cayenne pepper. Once the bacon is flipped, brush it with the maple syrup–brown sugar mixture and cook for another 5 minutes. Flip the bacon again and brush it with the mixture. Continue to cook for another 10 to 12 minutes, until golden brown, lacquered, and crispy. Remove the bacon from the EGG immediately and place on butcher paper to completely cool to room temperature.

LIBATIONS

(ADULTS ONLY)

Enjoying a great cocktail can signify many things: a celebration, a barbecue, a holiday, a wedding, a birthday, an anniversary, or maybe just 7:31 p.m. on a Tuesday night. The adult beverages in this chapter have all been grilled, smoked, or charred on the EGG. You can imagine how this creates tons of FLAVOR and adds a whole new dimension to these drinks. They range from cocktails to punch to sangria. So whether you're enjoying a drink by yourself or toasting with a fun-loving group of family and friends, look no further than this chapter. Note one side effect is that guests may not want to leave your house . . . Yeah . . . these libations are pretty delightful. Cheers!!

Grilled Watermelon Sangria

Makes about 8 servings

Patio, porch, or backyard, there's always something so refreshing about sangria during the summertime. Fresh seasonal fruit and wine—what more do you need? Well, I can think of a couple things: ripe summer seedless watermelon charred on the EGG and juiced, smoky bourbon, and a nice Argentinian Tempranillo red wine with flavors of blackberry and fig. You, too, can learn to make this thirst-quenching sangria. Just keep on reading . . .

SIMPLE SYRUP

1 cup granulated sugar

1 cup water

GARNISH

1 Granny Smith apple, skin on, small diced

1 medium orange, skin on, small diced

12 seedless red grapes, quartered

½ medium-sized seedless watermelon, cut in ½-inch wedges (rind removed)

SANGRIA

3 1-inch seedless medium-sized watermelon slices (rind removed)

1 (750-mL) bottle Tempranillo wine

1 cup bourbon

1 cup simple syrup

1 cup bottled orange juice

Juice of ½ lime

To make the simple syrup on the stovetop, in a small saucepot, add the sugar and water and bring to a boil. Remove from the stovetop and cool to room temperature. The syrup will keep refrigerated for up to 2 weeks.

To make the garnish, add all of the ingredients except the watermelon wedges to a medium bowl and combine until well mixed. Set aside.

Prepare the EGG to cook direct at 450°F. To make the sangria, place the watermelon slices and the watermelon wedges (for garnish) on the EGG cooking grid and grill for about 5 minutes on each side, or until charred. Remove the watermelon from the EGG and reserve the watermelon wedges for garnish. Blend watermelon slices (for sangria) in a food processor, until juiced. Pour the watermelon juice into a glass pitcher. Add the wine, bourbon, simple syrup, orange juice, and lime juice and whisk until well incorporated.

To serve, fill a glass halfway with ice, pour in the sangria, top with a heaping spoonful of fruit garnish, and place a grilled watermelon wedge on the rim of the glass.

Charred Pineapple Margarita

Makes 2 cocktails

Who says you gotta wait for Taco Tuesday to enjoy a margarita? I'm telling you right now I'm making and drinking these charred pineapple margaritas every day that ends with the letter "y"! They're that good. Charring the pineapple really concentrates the sweetness of the fruit and gives a nice smoky flavor that works very well with a quality reposado or añejo tequila. The lime juice provides much-need acidity to cut through the sweetness of the pineapple and agave nectar.

½ whole fresh pineapple, peeled, cored, and quartered

6 ounces reposado or añejo tequila

Juice from ½ lime

1 ounce agave nectar

2 lime wedges, for garnish

2 pineapple wedges, for garnish

Prepare the EGG to cook direct at 450°F. Place the pineapple on the EGG cooking grid and char all sides, about 4 minutes per side, or until browned and grill marks appear. Reserve 2 of the 4 pineapple wedges for garnish. Place the other 2 pineapple wedges in a food processor and blend until puréed. Measure ⅓ cup pineapple purée and transfer it to a cocktail shaker. Add the tequila, lime juice, and agave. Add ice to two 16-ounce rocks glasses. Dry shake the cocktail, then double strain into each glass. Garnish each with a lime wedge and a pineapple wedge.

Maple Smoked Old-Fashioned

Makes 2 cocktails

The traditional recipe for an old-fashioned cocktail is pretty hard to top. It's a classic cocktail that has stood the test of time—and Prohibition—and it still tastes great. The original drink has three simple ingredients: rye whiskey or bourbon, Angostura bitters, and sugar. Perfection! But what if I told you that you could make a maple smoked old-fashioned on the EGG? Okay, okay . . . Calm down. I'll tell you how . . .

1 cup cherry or apple wood chips, soaked for 1 hour in 2 cups water

2 cups ice

6 ounces of bourbon

4 dashes of Angostura orange bitters

1 ounce maple syrup

2 large ice cubes

Luxardo maraschino cherries, for garnish

2 orange twists, for garnish

Prepare the EGG to smoke at 300°F. Drain the wood chips and place them in the EGG over the hot coals. Add the ice to a deep aluminum half pan. In a cocktail shaker add the bourbon, bitters, and maple syrup and stir until incorporated (do not add ice). Divide the bourbon mixture between two highball glasses and then set them on the ice in the pan. Immediately place the pan on the EGG cooking grid and close the rEGGulator cap for 60 seconds to smoke the cocktails. Remove the cocktails from the EGG.

Place a large ice cube in each glass. Garnish each with a cherry and rub the orange twist on the rim of each glass, then drop it in.

Charred Grapefruit–Jalapeño Bourbon Sour

Makes 2 cocktails

When in doubt, sweet and spicy is always a good call! Charred bittersweet ruby red grapefruit, jalapeño simple syrup, and bourbon . . . I can already taste it! The blistering of the jalapeño really complements the smoky notes of the bourbon and the charred grapefruit. The acidity of the citrus is what brightens the cocktail, awakens the palate, and gives the drink a clean finish. It's got just the right amount of spicy kick to it.

SIMPLE SYRUP

2 medium jalapeños

1 cup water

1 cup granulated sugar

JUICE

1 large ruby red grapefruit, cut in half

1 medium lime, cut in half

COCKTAIL

8 ounces bourbon

1 ounce Cointreau

2 ounces jalapeño simple syrup

Juice of ½ lime

2 grapefruit peels, for garnish

Prepare the EGG to cook direct at 450°F. To make the simple syrup, place the jalapeños on the EGG cooking grid for 8 to 10 minutes, until lightly blistered all over. Remove them from the EGG and let cool. Once cool enough to handle, slice the jalapeños in half, keeping the seeds in only one pepper and removing the seeds in the other. If you prefer to make the syrup spicier, keep the seeds in both. Place a medium cast-iron saucepot on the EGG cooking grid and add the water, sugar, and jalapeños. Bring to a boil and cook for 3 to 5 minutes. Strain and set aside. The syrup will keep refrigerated for up to 2 weeks.

Meanwhile, to make the juice, place the grapefruit and lime on the EGG cooking grid, meat side down, and grill for about 5 minutes, or until charred. Squeeze the juice of the fruit into a cocktail shaker.

To make the cocktails, add the bourbon, Cointreau, simple syrup, and lime juice to the shaker. Add ice to two 16-ounce rocks glasses and rub the grapefruit peels on the rims of the glasses, and drop them in. Dry shake the cocktail, then strain into each glass.

Jamaican Rum Punch

Makes 8 to 10 servings

Jamaican rum punch . . . the official cocktail of Jamaica. What more can I say about it than we've had some great times together?! I guarantee this tropical rum punch will resurrect any gathering or barbecue party. Rum, fruit juices, Jamaican strawberry syrup, and my own personal twist to the classic recipe: a ginger simple syrup, because Jamaicans love ginger. But don't let the smooth taste fool you; this cocktail has Jamaican overproof rum in it, so it has a tendency to sneak up on you. So kick your feet up poolside and indulge in the Jamaican rum punch.

GINGER SYRUP

¼ cup peeled and sliced fresh ginger root

1 cup water

1 cup granulated sugar

PUNCH

1 cup Wray & Nephew Jamaican overproof rum

1 cup spiced Jamaican dark rum

2 cups orange juice

2 cups pineapple juice

½ cup ginger syrup

⅛ cup Jamaican strawberry syrup

Juice of 1 whole medium lime

Orange, lime, and pineapple slices, for garnish

Prepare the EGG to cook direct at 400°F. To make the ginger syrup, place a small cast-iron saucepot on the EGG cooking grid and add all of the ingredients. Bring to a boil, then continue to cook for 3 to 4 minutes. Remove the saucepot from the EGG and let the syrup cool. Remove the slices of ginger from the syrup and discard. Any leftover syrup can be stored and refrigerated for up to 2 weeks.

For the punch, combine all of the ingredients in a large pitcher and stir until fully incorporated. Pour over ice and garnish with slices of orange, lime, and pineapple.

CHAPTER

8

HAPPY ENDING

(DESSERT)

Every story deserves a happy ending, and *EGGin'* is no different. Sweet treats and smoked desserts are the perfect conclusion to any meal because the Big Green Egg really can do it all! Custardy Jamaican rum–raisin bread pudding and a bourbon and ginger-laced smoked pecan pie are just a few of the treasures you'll find in this chapter. Baking on the EGG adds a nice smoky-savory note that gives a complex depth to each dessert. Smoking with pecan, apple, or cherry wood chips is a great option when EGGin' any of these recipes. These desserts are the proper ending to our EGGin' fairy tale, and I'm fairly certain they will help put you right to sleep to dream about the next time . . .

Grilled Pound Cake
with Myers's Rum Cream Sauce
and Blueberry Sauce

Makes 6 to 8 servings

You forgot to make or purchase a dessert for your barbecue. Don't fret! I got you covered, fellow EGGheads. This is a quick and delicious dessert that you can whip up in no time. All you need is a store-bought pound cake, some blueberries, and a couple of bottles of alcohol. Grilling the pound cake on the EGG warms up the cake and gives it a nice contrast in texture. The Myers's rum cream sauce gives this dessert the "yum factor." And the pound cake is like a sponge that wants to soak up all that good sauce!

BLUEBERRY SAUCE

1 cup peach schnapps

Juice and finely grated zest from
1 medium navel orange

½ cup granulated sugar

1 pound fresh blueberries

CREAM SAUCE

1½ cups Myers's dark rum

1 cup heavy cream

½ cup granulated sugar

Seeds from 1 vanilla bean

Pinch of kosher salt

WHIPPED CREAM

1 cup heavy cream

2 tablespoons confectioners' sugar

1 (11.5-ounce) pound cake

Vegetable oil, for oiling the
cooking grid

8 ounces chopped salted,
roasted pistachios

Prepare the EGG to cook direct at 400°F. To make the blueberry sauce, place a medium cast-iron saucepot on the EGG cooking grid and add the peach schnapps, orange juice and zest, and sugar. Bring to a boil, then add the blueberries. Continue to cook for 6 to 8 minutes, until the sauce thickens and the blueberries become tender and glazed. Remove the pot from the EGG and set aside to cool the sauce to room temperature.

To make the cream sauce, place a large cast-iron saucepot on the EGG cooking grid and add the rum. Cook for 2 to 3 minutes, until reduced by half. Add the heavy cream, sugar, vanilla seeds, and salt. Continue to cook for 3 to 4 minutes, until the sauce reaches the consistency of caramel. Remove the saucepot from the EGG.

To make the whipped cream, chill a medium stainless-steel bowl in the freezer for 15 minutes. Add the heavy cream and confectioners' sugar and, using an electric hand mixer on medium-high speed, whip until stiff peaks form. Cover the bowl with plastic wrap and refrigerate until ready to use.

Slice the pound cake into 1½-inch slices. Oil the EGG cooking grid with vegetable oil to prevent sticking. Place the pound cake on the EGG and grill for 1 to 2 minutes per side, until warmed and grill marks form. Remove the pound cake from the EGG.

To serve, spoon some cream sauce on the plate first and top with a piece of pound cake. Top the cake with a spoonful of the blueberry sauce and a dollop of whipped cream, then finish with crushed pistachios and serve.

Bourbon–Ginger Pecan Pie

Makes 8 servings

There is no other dessert more Southern than pecan pie. It's sticky, it's nutty, it's sweet, and it has a mild savory note. Whether you pronounce it "pee-can" or "pah-cahn," here's one thing we can all agree on . . . This bourbon–ginger pecan pie is drool-worthy. With a little bit of bourbon and a splash of ginger liquor . . . "Houston we have liftoff!" The good thing is it's still kid-friendly because the alcohol cooks off when you bake it. The bad thing is the kids will probably eat it all and not save you any. But you have the recipe now, so make two pies. Problem solved!

1 cup pecan wood chips, soaked for
    1 hour in 2 cups water

FILLING

1 cup dark corn syrup

1 tablespoon molasses

4 large eggs, beaten

2 tablespoons butter, melted

Seeds from 1 vanilla bean

2 tablespoons bourbon

1 tablespoon Domaine de Canton
    ginger liquor

¾ cup granulated sugar

¼ teaspoon kosher salt

1 (9-inch) unbaked or frozen
    deep-dish pie crust

1½ cups coarsely chopped
    roasted pecans

EGG WASH

1 medium egg

1 teaspoon water

Fresh whipped cream or
    vanilla ice cream, for serving

Prepare the EGG to cook indirect with a drip pan at 375°F. Drain the wood chips and place them in the EGG over the hot coals. In a medium bowl, add the corn syrup, molasses, eggs, butter, vanilla seeds, bourbon, ginger liquor, sugar, and salt and whisk until fully incorporated.

If frozen, thaw the pie crust for 10 minutes. Then spread the pecans evenly over the bottom of the pie crust. Carefully pour the liquid mixture over the pecans.

In a small bowl, whisk together the egg and water. Brush the pie crust edges with the egg wash.

Bake the pie in the EGG for 35 to 40 minutes, until the sides puff up and the center barely jiggles. Remove from the EGG and let cool for 2 to 3 hours. Serve with whipped cream or ice cream.

Jamaican Rum–Raisin Bread Pudding

Makes 8 to 10 servings

Rum raisin is an extremely popular Jamaican ice cream flavor, and we are serious about our bread pudding—very serious. I like to poach the raisins in rum, to infuse some of that booziness, and then fold the poached raisins into the bread pudding . . . and then pour some of that rum-raisin glaze on top of the hot bread pudding the second it leaves the EGG. Feel free to finish it off with rum raisin or vanilla ice cream. Either way you can't lose.

2 cups spiced Jamaican dark rum

1 cup granulated sugar

1 cup golden raisins

10 cups white bread, with crust (about 14 slices), cut in 1-inch cubes

8 large eggs

1½ cups heavy cream

1½ cups packed dark brown sugar

1 teaspoon ground cinnamon

Seeds from 1 vanilla bean

Pinch of kosher salt

2 tablespoons unsalted butter

Vanilla ice cream, for serving

Prepare the EGG to cook direct at 400°F. Place a medium cast-iron saucepot on the cooking grid of the EGG, add the rum and sugar. Bring to a boil, then add the raisins and continue cooking for about 8 minutes, or until slightly syrupy. Remove the saucepot from the EGG, and reserve half of the raisins from the glaze and place in a small bowl. Set the saucepot and the bowl aside.

Place the bread in a large bowl. In a separate medium bowl, add the eggs, heavy cream, brown sugar, cinnamon, vanilla seeds, and salt and whisk until well incorporated. Add the custard mixture and reserved drained raisins to the bread. Use a rubber spatula to fold and incorporate everything together, until all of the bread cubes are moistened.

Prepare the EGG to cook indirect with a drip pan at 400°F. Rub the butter on the bottom and sides of a 12-inch cast-iron pan and pour in the bread and custard mixture. Use a spatula to flatten the surface. Let the bread pudding sit for 20 to 30 minutes, to allow the bread to completely absorb the custard. Place the pan in the EGG and bake the bread pudding for 35 to 40 minutes, until the edges and top are golden brown and a toothpick comes out clean.

Reheat the reserved rum-raisin glaze and pour over the warm bread pudding. Allow bread pudding to cool for 12 to 15 minutes before slicing into it. Serve with ice cream.

Smoked Sweet Potato Cheesecake

Makes 8 to 10 servings

I'm all about multitasking, and that's why I combined these two desserts for one sensational bite. The natural sweetness from the sweet potatoes blends nicely with the smooth mouthfeel of the cream cheese and a gingersnap crust. Whipped sweet potato and vanilla bean together just make me happy. You'll want to put this one in your dessert repertoire!

CHEESECAKE

1½ pounds sweet potatoes

24 ounces cream cheese, at room temperature

¼ cup heavy cream

Seeds from 2 vanilla beans

3 large eggs

1 (14-ounce) can sweetened condensed milk

8 ounces gingersnap cookies (about 28 to 30 cookies), finely blended in a food processor

4 tablespoons unsalted butter, melted

1 cup pecan wood chips, soaked for 1 hour in 2 cups water

Ice cream or fresh whipped cream, for serving (optional)

Prepare the EGG to cook indirect at 375°F. To make the cheesecake, wet the skin of the sweet potatoes and wrap them individually in aluminum foil. Place the sweet potatoes on the EGG cooking grid and roast for 45 to 60 minutes, until fork tender. Remove the sweet potatoes from the EGG, and remove the foil, cooling them slightly before peeling off the skin. Mash the sweet potatoes in a medium bowl until smooth, then transfer to the bowl of a stand mixer.

Using a stand mixer fitted with the whip attachment, whip the sweet potatoes until smooth and any lumps are gone. Add the cream cheese, heavy cream, vanilla seeds, eggs, and condensed milk. Whip for 2 to 3 minutes, until light and fluffy. Set aside.

To make the crust, in a medium bowl, combine the cookie crumbs and butter. Stir together until the texture resembles wet sand. Firmly press into the bottom of a 9-inch springform pan or on all sides of a tart pan with a removable bottom. Pour the cheesecake mixture on top of the crust; no need to blind-bake the crust first.

Prepare the EGG to cook indirect with a drip pan at 350°F. Drain the wood chips and place them in the EGG over the hot coals. Smoke the cheesecake for 45 to 60 minutes, until the sides are set and a toothpick comes out clean. Remove from the EGG and let cool. Place the cheesecake in the refrigerator overnight, or at least 3 hours. To serve, gently run a knife around the edge of the cheesecake to loosen it before removing the sides of the springform pan. Serve with ice cream or whipped cream.

Peach Crostata

Makes 8 servings

It's called a peach crostata in Italy and a peach galette in France. This freeform pie/tart is essentially the same thing in both countries. But it's indisputable that this classic dessert is a timeless favorite among people worldwide. I chose to make mine with Georgia peaches, since this is the state where I discovered my passion for being a chef. The peach crostata is as sweet as Atlanta was to me when I first moved here and as it continues to be in my career. I hope you enjoy it as much as I do!

1 cup pecan wood chips, soaked for 1 hour in 2 cups water

FILLING

1 pound fresh peaches, pits removed, thinly sliced ¼ inch thick

¼ cup packed light brown sugar

½ teaspoon ground cinnamon

1 tablespoon bourbon

Seeds from 1 vanilla bean

2 teaspoons cornstarch

1 premade refrigerated pie crust

EGG WASH

1 medium egg

1 teaspoon water

2 tablespoons turbinado sugar

Vanilla ice cream or fresh whipped cream, for serving (optional)

Prepare the EGG to cook indirect with a drip pan at 400°F. Drain the wood chips and place them in the EGG over the hot coals. To make the filling, combine the peaches, brown sugar, cinnamon, bourbon, vanilla seeds, and cornstarch in a large bowl and gently toss. Let the fruit macerate for 30 minutes at room temperature, allowing the flavors to penetrate the peaches.

Line a 15-inch pizza stone with parchment paper cut to size. Lay the pie crust on the pizza stone and gently roll out the crust 1 to 1½ inches from the edge, using a rolling pin. Lay the peaches in the middle of the pie crust in a very thin layer, about 3 inches away from the edge of the pie crust. Pour the remaining juices in the bowl over the peaches. Fold the edges of the pie crust about 2 inches up over the sides of the peaches.

In a small bowl, whisk together the egg and the water. Brush the pie crust edges with the egg wash and sprinkle with turbinado sugar.

Cook the crostata for 40 to 45 minutes, until golden brown and the peaches are tender and caramelized.

Allow the crostata to cool for 15 to 20 minutes, until it firms up, before slicing. It's traditionally eaten by itself, but if you prefer, feel free to serve with ice cream or fresh whipped cream.

Acknowledgments

Big Green Egg has always been like a family to me. To have *EGGin'* not only be my first cookbook but also a Big Green Egg cookbook is truly a dream come true! This book is a testament to the hard work and dedication of many people, and without them, this book wouldn't be possible. To Ed Fisher, the man behind the Big Green Egg, thank you for creating not only an amazing product but also a culture behind it. Thanks for your words of encouragement and positivity. To my Big Green Egg family: Ardy Arani, Jodi Burson, Bob Atkinson, Rob D'Amico, Jerry Stone, and everyone at "the Mothership," thank you for always supporting all of my grilling ventures near and far and having an open mind to my ideas.

Jean Lucas and Andrews McMeel, wow! We've definitely had some late nights and early mornings making sure that *EGGin'* was just right. Thank you for taking my recipes, vision, and culinary voice and making magic happen. Kathryn McCrary, thank you for your breathtaking food photography; your photos brought my food to life on these pages. Thank you, Thomas Driver, you're the man with the set design plan. Tamie Cook and Savannah Sasser, thank you for your amazing food styling. And last, but definitely not least, "Ms.T" Talisa Tarber and Tyran Cosby, thank you for always being there when I needed you two. This cookbook is for all the EGGheads across the globe! I hope you enjoy *EGGin'* and eating these recipes as much as I enjoyed creating them.

David with Ed Fisher

Metric Conversions and Equivalents

Metric Conversion Formulas

To Convert	Multiply
Ounces to grams	Ounces by 28.35
Pounds to kilograms	Pounds by .454
Teaspoons to milliliters	Teaspoons by 4.93
Tablespoons to milliliters	Tablespoons by 14.79
Fluid ounces to milliliters	Fluid ounces by 29.57
Cups to milliliters	Cups by 236.59
Cups to liters	Cups by .236
Pints to liters	Pints by .473
Quarts to liters	Quarts by .946
Gallons to liters	Gallons by 3.785
Inches to centimeters	Inches by 2.54

Common Ingredients and Their Approximate Equivalents

1 cup uncooked white rice = 185 grams
1 cup all-purpose flour = 125 grams
1 stick butter (4 ounces • ½ cup • 8 tablespoons) = 115 grams
1 cup butter (8 ounces • 2 sticks • 16 tablespoons) = 225 grams
1 cup brown sugar (firmly packed) = 220 grams
1 cup granulated sugar = 200 grams

Oven Temperatures

To convert Fahrenheit to Celsius, subtract 32 from Fahrenheit, multiply the result by 5, then divide by 9.

Description	Fahrenheit	Celsius	British Gas Mark
Very cool	200°	95°	0
Very cool	225°	110°	¼
Very cool	250°	120°	½
Cool	275°	135°	1
Cool	300°	150°	2
Warm	325°	165°	3
Moderate	350°	175°	4
Moderately hot	375°	190°	5
Fairly hot	400°	200°	6
Hot	425°	220°	7
Very hot	450°	230°	8
Very hot	475°	245°	9

Approximate Metric Equivalents

Volume

¼ teaspoon	1 milliliter
½ teaspoon	2.5 milliliters
¾ teaspoon	4 milliliters
1 teaspoon	5 milliliters
1¼ teaspoons	6 milliliters
1½ teaspoons	7.5 milliliters
1¾ teaspoons	8.5 milliliters
2 teaspoons	10 milliliters
1 tablespoon (½ fluid ounce)	15 milliliters
2 tablespoons (1 fluid ounce)	30 milliliters
¼ cup	60 milliliters
⅓ cup	80 milliliters
½ cup (4 fluid ounces)	120 milliliters
⅔ cup	160 milliliters
¾ cup	180 milliliters
1 cup (8 fluid ounces)	240 milliliters
1¼ cups	300 milliliters
1½ cups (12 fluid ounces)	360 milliliters
1⅔ cups	400 milliliters
2 cups (1 pint)	460 milliliters
3 cups	700 milliliters
4 cups (1 quart)	0.95 liter
1 quart plus ¼ cup	1 liter
4 quarts (1 gallon)	3.8 liters

Weight

¼ ounce	7 grams
½ ounce	14 grams
¾ ounce	21 grams
1 ounce	28 grams
1¼ ounces	35 grams
1½ ounces	42.5 grams
1⅔ ounces	45 grams
2 ounces	57 grams
3 ounces	85 grams
4 ounces (¼ pound)	113 grams
5 ounces	142 grams
6 ounces	170 grams
7 ounces	198 grams
8 ounces (½ pound)	227 grams
16 ounces (1 pound)	454 grams
35.25 ounces (2.2 pounds)	1 kilogram

Length

⅛ inch	3 millimeters
¼ inch	6 millimeters
½ inch	12 millimeters
1 inch	2.5 centimeters
2 inches	5 centimeters
2½ inches	6 centimeters
4 inches	10 centimeters
5 inches	13 centimeters
6 inches	15 centimeters
12 inches (1 foot)	30 centimeters

Information compiled from a variety of sources, including *Recipes into Type* by Joan Whitman and Dolores Simon (Newton, MA: Biscuit Books, 1993); *The New Food Lover's Companion* by Sharon Tyler Herbst (Hauppauge, NY: Barron's, 2013); and *Rosemary Brown's Big Kitchen Instruction Book* (Kansas City, MO: Andrews McMeel, 1998).

Index

Andrews McMeel Publishing
a division of Andrews McMeel Universal
1130 Walnut Street, Kansas City, Missouri 64106

Big Green Egg, EGG, The Ultimate Cooking Experience, EGGhead, EGGfest,
EGGcessories, EGGtoberfest, convEGGtor, rEGGulator, EGGniter, MiniMax EGG, Nest,
EGG Mates, and The Green Color are registered trademarks of The Big Green Egg, Inc.

www.andrewsmcmeel.com
www.chefdavidrose.com
www.biggreenegg.com

21 22 23 24 25 SDB 10 9 8 7 6 5 4 3 2 1

ISBN: 978-1-4494-8760-7

Library of Congress Control Number: 2021936745

Editor: Jean Z. Lucas
Art Director and Designer: Julie Barnes
Photographer: Kathryn McCrary
Food Stylist: Tamie Cook
Prop Stylist: Thom Driver
Photo Assistant: Tanner Lynn
Food Stylist Assistant: Savannah Sasser
Production Manager: Carol Coe
Production Editor: Amy Strassner

ATTENTION: SCHOOLS AND BUSINESSES
Andrews McMeel books are available at quantity discounts with bulk purchase
for educational, business, or sales promotional use. For information, please e-mail the
Andrews McMeel Publishing Special Sales Department: specialsales@amuniversal.com.